#BREAKTHROUGH

Unleash Your Remarkable Brand Value, Influence & Authority

By

Doyle Buehler

"Evolve Your Strategy & Marketing"

DOYLE BUEHLER

#BREAKTHROUGH

Unleash Your Remarkable Brand Value, Influence and Authority

#Breakthrough
Unleash Your Remarkable Brand Value, Influence & Authority

By Doyle Buehler

Published by Dept.Digital (US)
Tampa, Florida, United States of America 2018

Visit book/author website: www.breakthrough.digital
Visit publishers website: www.Dept.Digital
Email: doyle@dept.digital

Author: Buehler, Doyle Robert, 1969-
Title: #Breakthrough: Unleash Your Remarkable Brand Value, Influence & Authority

ISBN
978-0-9996479-0-5 (Ppbk – #Breakthrough)
978-0-9996479-1-2 (eBook – #Breakthrough)

Subjects:

Buehler, Doyle
Social Selling
Branding
Internet Marketing
Social Media
Web Site Design
Content Marketing
Business Strategy

Dewey Number: 658.872

Words of Praise for #Breakthrough

"Buehler invites us along as he travels up the various digital tributaries into the mystical heart of darkness that is the digital industry, where we encounter the monkey and reptilian tribes that inhabit these parts and the digital extremists, false gurus and the downright rogues that lead them. He then systematically asks us to recognise the selfperpetuating fraud that is the norm here and brings some real light into the otherwise heated, cluttered and confusing world of online. It was well worth the trip."

John Lynch
Entrepreneur
Climbing Fish Ltd, Digital Ministry

"Most entrepreneurs still have their heads in the sand when it comes to their online strategy and Doyle pulls no punches with this book as he offers a proven methodology for driving serious results online."

Glen Carlson
CEO
Key Person Of Influence Australia

"Let online expert Doyle Buehler be your coach and guide through the world of digital marketing. Practical, down to earth, and full of "how-to" advice, this book will help you become the leader in your field or industry."

Matthew Michalewicz
Author of Life in a Half Second
www.Michalewicz.com.au

"There is so much misinformation and downright confusion about the online world; thank goodness someone has finally written the book to make sense of it all. Doyle Buehler gives all the right information, delivered in a no BS way, that is the key to actually making the most of the online world and social media in any business."

Andrew Griffiths
Australia's #1 Small Business and Entrepreneurial Author.

#BREAKTHROUGH

Unleash Your Remarkable Brand Value, Influence & Authority

By

Doyle Buehler

" *There is no reason anyone would want a personal computer in their home.* *"*

- Ken Olson,
Digital Equipment founder, 1977

INCLUDES FREE ENTREPRENEURS
ONLINE TRAINING COURSE

Get the exclusive Digital Strategy Training course for readers only.
Over 20+ hours of content and $367 in value.
Email bonus@breakthrough.digital for complete course access now.

DOWNLOAD THE FREE PDF VERSION OF #BREAKTHROUGH

Get a digital PDF copy for your smartphone, tablet or ebook reader.
Go to breakthrough.digital/pdf to get your free copy now.

TABLE OF CONTENTS

TABLE OF CONTENTS

TABLE OF CONTENTS

TABLE OF CONTENTS

THE STATUS QUO

My Digital Journey So Far

Working in the online and e-commerce world for over 14 years, from the very early days of being online in an ecommerce start-up, has taught me some key principles and understandings. I have come through the entire evolution of online growth and change – from the original brochure websites (that sadly still exist today) to high-level social media marketing campaigns and everything in between.

There have been many marketing campaigns and online strategies in which I can see what works. Not just what works, but what once worked and what doesn't work anymore. I have seen what's starting to work, and in the future what will work. I am so close to this online realm that I know all the history and also intuitively seem to know what is coming up next (but alas, not always 'right' either).

I have failed with many things online, as well as having some successes; I have worked with some massively big companies, like Samsung, Virgin Mobile, Toshiba, Skoda, Suzuki, Blackmores, and created one of the fastest growing online companies in Canada. All of this has helped me understand what we can deliver, but also the disconnect that exists online.

The problem with most businesses online is that they get so caught up doing the day-to-day "things" to run their business, which they seem to forget that they are in the most technologically, revolutionary time in history. This is in fact the digital revolution. The technology overwhelms them, and, they simply forget that most of the tools online are designed

The Digital Revolution is here. Are you ready?
Image courtesy of Tom Burns: everythingburns.com

to help businesses get the word out and spread their marketing information directly to the marketplace – their audience. You have probably heard it before, but most business owners are working "in" the business; whereas the transformation to a business leader or entrepreneur, means that you work "on" your business.

More importantly, the biggest problem is that many entrepreneurs are not quite sure what they don't know, and what they need to be doing, so they simply ignore it. This turns into a huge problem for businesses.

They get caught in the clutter online and need to do something to break through to their audience.

I find it so frustrating to see businesses flounder today, as they miss tremendous opportunities in front of them. They could be doing so much more. Or, alternatively, they get drawn into a short-term solution, an overnight "fix" that further moves them backwards.

It's been said that there are thousands of email marketers, Internet marketers, online gurus, SEO wizards, and all that sort of stuff, and that it's simply not worth paying any attention to them. It's true that in every industry there is good and bad. The underlying truth is that we are going through a massive transformation, and some people will benefit, and some will not. There are good people who will help you benefit and there are those who won't.

The real reason behind this book and everything else I do is that I have a passion for businesses that operate in the digital space, along with marketing, and of course the strategies that make it all work.

I constantly think about digital innovation and entrepreneurship, and how we can make things better for all businesses. With my entrepreneurial background, I could have taken my passion and channelled it into absolutely any field and any industry that I enjoyed and loved. However, when I really analyzed and realized what this transforming technology was moving ahead to do, I understood that small businesses were the hottest place where this was going to happen. This is "the" place for an incredible opportunity and the ground zero for the biggest impact for all things entrepreneurial. There has never been a better time for a business to deliver their remarkable product to their perfect audience, online.

I wanted to be right there, to see and watch people's faces light up when they "get it," when they realize that it now changes their life and their business. When they see that "ah-ha" moment that makes revolutionary and transformational changes for them, then things start to fall in place, and they then understand how this will change their lives and the lives of those around them.

The mission for me is not about the software, not about the tools, not about the social media, or the techno-babble of it all; it's about seeing people reach that moment when they realize how everything comes together. I believe that this stuff has the capability to free up people's time. If we all have more time, we can all be more successful, and then we can really start tackling the bigger problems that need attention.

I want to educate people on what is going on in the online world. This book is designed to do just that - give you and your business an extra hand for you to "get it"; for you to truly put everything in place with what your original business dream was all about.

I am known for making complex online digital systems and strategies easy to use and simple to understand; systems that are suitable and simple for small businesses to implement. From interacting with this strategy, people are left feeling like they are in fact building a breakthrough - a true online empire builder.

The development of this overall digital strategy for this book was multi-fold. For awhile, when someone would ask for help or assistance in search engine optimization, paid search advertising, social media, website development, or whatever it was that they needed, they would always seem to have their blinders on for how everything actually fit together and how all aspects linked and worked together. Many questions were raised, and nothing was connected. But to everyone, it seemed as though that was ok, that it didn't really matter. From these large false "assumptions" that a lot of businesses live throughout, I coined the expression, the 'Seven Deadly Digital Delusions', to help us get pointed in the right direction, and help fill in the gaps for what is really important to not only start, but to keep on going.

Doyle Buehler

There are a lot of books on the shelves of thousands of bookstores, and millions of book owners of these same books. There is no shortage of books about online business, SEO this, online marketing, Social Media that... e-commerce here, adwords there. "Dummies" everywhere it seems.

The most significant thing that really came to mind that was missing from all of these books, was organization and order – strategies that could be formulated across your entire digital ecosystem. Too many books are all over the place, with little focus on the core problem. The core issue was always diluted with technologies and babble – not the foundation of what is needed to actually build a strong business. Others continue to perpetuate the delusion with information that is irrelevant, out of context, and has no simple framework to keep all the different pieces fitting together.

I almost always felt more confused after reading these sorts of books. There is obviously a need for these different levels of books, as they do help in specific cases – there just wasn't anything that actually tied this all together. All of this is about to change right now with this book. The delusions are definitely real - but more importantly how you can overcome them to become the leader in your industry.

I want to connect leaders to digital. To enable them; to give them the tools, resources, and knowledge to make a difference with their business. This is why I wrote this book.

I want to help you build that strategic alignment and online integration as well, so you and your business can reach spectacular growth. This is why I created the strategies, the framework, and communicating it through the story of developing a breakthrough online for your business. Once you have implemented and mastered this process, you will be able to do what you love - grow and dominate with your business.

Enjoy discovering your digital leadership, building your influence and revealing your new reality, to get to your breakthrough online

Doyle Buehler

www.breakthrough.digital

I BOUGHT INTO MEDIOCRITY. HAVE YOU?

What This Book Will Help You Solve

We're all wasting our time online - yes, you too (and me!).

We've lost our focus on what is really important about business online.

We're not really sure what to do next, either.

And, how do you break through and create influence online? How do you get a thriving audience base, and of course more orders or sales?

And, we've been misled as well. It's not about "traffic"; it's not about "followers" either. Yet, we're "told" that this is the holy grail of online. It's not, and I will show you why. The solution to getting a breakthrough is much much deeper than that.

And, it's not just about being on Facebook either. Despite taking so many courses on SEO, Facebook training, workshops, and learning how to run a group on Linkedin, or setting up a small website, many businesses still cannot get any traction online.

I have spent over 15 years in the online, e-commerce worlds, including start-ups, media agencies and everything in between. I have developed many online systems, including developing online strategies, advertising campaigns, social media activities, community building, and everything else. I have seen what works and what doesn't. I have seen what some companies truly understand, and where other companies are simply missing the point.

I know how much it can hurt, and even made all the mistakes myself. I started an ecommerce business in Canada in 2002. The web was still pretty new. Facebook didn't exist. Neither did Linkedin. Twitter was still just a dream. Annoying SEO sales people? Thankfully, not yet.

I was pretty naïve. I made every mistake in the book (if there even was one that was written at the time). We developed an incredible customer-centric design studio, that would rival Canva, even today. Hard coded in Flash, it was the envy of all ...in 2004. And, it cost over $250,000 to develop. Yet, it was just a website. Just a tool. Not a business - not even close.

We discovered the hard way that this was not going to work all alone and that we needed to do something quickly to actually make it work, to develop a business that worked for the long-term. Despite the heartaches and costs, we started to connect the dots. We started to get all the pieces together into a viable business, into an ecosystem that connected everything together.

How? We started from basics and looked at the overall strategy and the value that we were delivering to each and every customer. We eventually got the pieces working together: we were named the "Top 50 Fastest Growing Companies" in Canada in 2008, followed by "The #1 Fastest Growing Company" in the state, in 2008. We had also licensed the design and manufacturing web technology to companies around the world.

What did I discover since these crazy days of a start-up? Simply, that there are significant pieces that are just missing from what should be done online.

This is your guide to setting it up properly for the first time or making sure that you are truly running things online, the way they should be, for an existing business.

Doyle Buehler

Many businesses are simply unable to put the pieces together, so they work each problem in isolation of the inter-connectedness of everything else, hoping that it will work. It's not because they are not 'smart' either, as we all know that entrepreneurs excel; it's because the industry has become so complicated and has created pillars or silos of expertise that are so hard to break into and break out of this thinking.

This simply doesn't work.

Simply, put, what has been lacking in businesses online?

1. A solid strategy that encapsulates everything that is done online, and ties together their entire digital ecosystem
2. An understanding of what is really important about marketing and online business
3. An understanding of how to tie all of the different parts of online together into a cohesive brand "ecosystem" - social media, content, websites, landing pages, advertising, visuals, analytics.

How do you juggle the complexities of working "on" your business, as well as working "in" your business?

What did I discover about online that helped pull all these pieces together?

The key to getting a breakthrough and online success is simplicity.

It's about developing a process or methodology that allows you to focus on what is really important, and identify that which is just a "buzz," for you to avoid. The real power is how you connect your entire digital ecosystem, of everything that you do and say and deliver your value-driven message.

It is about setting priorities for you and your business, so you know what to do, and more importantly, when.

Currently, when you start a business or grow it online, you are expected to do certain things - starting with a website. Did you know that this is where most businesses fail, that simply put up a website?

A website does not make a business. Nor should you actually 'start' with a website, either. While not the 'last' step, it is not as big a priority as most think; I'll tell you why.

What is the real purpose of the website? Leads? Sales? You'd be surprised to know that 98% of websites are not actually designed to generate leads or sales for business, but rather just to "show off". They have no real Return on Investment (ROI).

Yes, a business needs a website, but it also needs something more important - a solid strategy of the 'why', the value that you will deliver, the importance of your customer. A business without a strategy will never find focus in what they do and what they deliver. This is where you need to start.

This is where this book starts and continues to the end, to get all of the pieces aligned properly with your overall online objectives.

It is true that some businesses are "working it" and "working it well" online. If you are like the rest, you have probably wondered exactly how they are doing it right, or why it is actually working for them.

The difference? They have a system, a platform, and a framework; a framework that puts everything that they do into context and shows the relative importance of each aspect.

This book is about building your systems, your methodologies, your frameworks, your platform to deliver your exceptional value, online.

Doyle Buehler

What I have found, and what has been quite predominant is that the companies that are making online strategies "work" for them are the companies that can integrate all the different segments of an online strategy. They have been able to put the different pieces together, despite the seemingly varied nature of them. This is what this book is about - providing a clear picture of what is needed, and further creating a defining framework that allows the business leader to triumph online. This is what digital strategy is about. These are what I call the 7 Disciplines of Digital Leadership - the concepts that tie together the "must have" information that you need.

This is what I call digital leadership, and this is what this book shows you how to improve. At the end of the day, it is not just about doing things; it is more about showing things. How you demonstrate your digital leadership will show how you demonstrate your true industry expertise for your audience.

This book outlines the methods for achieving success online, based on these core problems - by helping you build a sound strategy that is based on years of work in the field. And, it is based on real-world experience of getting all the pieces to work like a concerto.

By reading and understanding this framework, you will be able to gain additional traction, and move more of your ideal audience into your sales funnel for additional sales and business growth.

This book will help you "tweak" things to becoming a fine running machine. It will show you what you need to continue to build your audience, as well as make you aware of critical aspects that you may be missing.

This digital strategy is simply called the **Breakthrough Digital Business** Framework, and was designed from the ground up to address the common mistakes that are being made by most businesses online. It will detail the best way to create integration across all of the many areas of online business that exist.

Everything that entrepreneurs need to know to build their business has been condensed into a unique, 7 step process that will create the change that you are looking for, for your business. While the process created is meant to be somewhat linear and consecutive so that entrepreneurs can walk through each day, day by day, you are also able to jump into the framework at any time and at any stage, depending on the maturity of your business. That being said, completing each step or day in a consecutive fashion, allows you to truly build on the knowledge base that the previous day enabled.

You may be starting to get your orientation in what needs to be done. You want some action to happen. You want things to grow. You want to get to that tipping point or create the momentum that will build a business breakthrough. You want to be the leading business that people will come to when they want to deal with someone. While this will certainly help in creating some realignment to your core business, it is also a reflection on what everyone needs to address in growing their business to the next level and building the business breakthrough that is out there.

Any online business is no different in essence than their bricks and mortar counterpart. It is about building customer relationships, having an understanding of what works and what doesn't, a framework to hold it all together, and a system to make it run. So how do I increase my level of success online?

Many businesses expect some miraculous moment where everything will suddenly be relevant. "Maybe that video of the cat that was posted last week will go "viral" or maybe those hilarious photos of the bacon that were posted last month will finally make a difference". Or they think Facebook will be the solution to all their problems.

Fact: there is no magic bullet, miracles don't happen in the online world, and Facebook does not bring salvation. Great things happen online only when you know and understand what is important to your business, and your industry, and leverage that knowledge in order to create an online strategy. No one can create a better online strategy for you, other than yourself. This is the essence of digital strategy.

The ideas in this book will help get you to where you want, but ultimately you need to be the leader - the digital leader. Yes, your business needs an online strategy that you will get from this book – but first, it needs a champion. You are that champion; by understanding how to overcome these elements that are truly holding you back.

This is how you can build your online empire. Take the pieces that are critical to defining your 'why' and delivering your value to your online audience. This is how you achieve success. This is what you will find here.

Who Is This Book For?

This book is for business leaders, business owners, entrepreneurs and forward thinkers who are ready to move their business to the next level. It is about bringing on your A-game online. It's about delivering your remarkable value; about building your business!

This book will also help **innovative marketers** who want to be able to pull all of the different aspects of digital into a smooth running platform that helps you manage and navigate it all.

It will help **entrepreneurs and business owners** pare down what is really important, and help you sort through the clutter and confusion of everything that you "should" be doing, to give you the time and resources to focus 'on' your business.

It will assist **startups** with designing a systematized platform to launch their products and services, so they can focus on and capitalize on the product itself, not worrying about how to put the digital pieces together.

And, it will help **CDOs**, **CMOs** and other **Strategic & Marketing Leaders** create a strategic system and workflow that can be used by your team to scale and grow the business, methodically, without the headaches of multiple and sometimes disjointed goals between skills and departments.

Is This Book Right For You?

This book is not for everybody. If you want to understand the key concepts that will help you pull all of the pieces together into a solid, comprehensive digital strategy, this book will provide the instructions and the tools to do this. You will learn how to take all of the disparate parts of online, and create a comprehensive, simple platform that provides you with priorities and focus.

Digital strategy and true digital leadership is the "long-game" of online. If you are looking for a one-hit-wonder, or wanting to create that viral post that will get you 10 million views tomorrow, generating Internet Billions, or creating that "New, 7 Figure income while you sleep" program, then this book is definitely not for you.

If you want to take what you already know about online, refine it, get rid of the fluff, and ensure that it all works together for you, smoothly, then this book will take you there. It will give you the tools, the understanding and the knowledge of what you can actually do, and do well.

In this book, you will create a long-term breakthrough by learning:

1. How to create a compelling digital strategy that will answer the compelling question of 'why' and how you will deliver remarkable value online.
2. What is important about online marketing and how to properly use it for your specific requirements.

3. How to build a strong, stable platform for your own digital ecosystem, by utilizing a simple methodology.

4. How to prioritize what is important online, and what is simply a distraction to your business.

5. How to design your product funnels to create long-term interest in what you do.

6. How to nurture your audience from disinterested observer to committed client

7. How to grow your online profile that tells people how you dominate your business niche.

8. How to become the digital leader - the person who can become the champion of online business development.

9. How to effectively connect and complement your digital ecosystem to create your breakthrough online with your business.

About The Format

This book is broken into three main parts.

Part 1: Understanding Your Digital Basics gives you the needed background information - "The Digital Basics". This helps you understand the principles of what is really important about online, and how it fits together.

Part 2: Online Implementation details out digital leadership through the exact Digital Business Breakthrough framework that you need, as well as a deeper understanding of the 'why' and the 'how'.

Part 3: Reboot Your Strategy is the wrap-up, where you can continue to understand the resources needed to better manage your breakthrough.

Notes On This Edition

This book was originally published in Australia as *'The Digital Delusion, How to Overcome the Misguidance & Misinformation Online'*. Otherwise known as the "Crowdfunding" edition, created by my Pozible Crowdfunding campaign in 2014. This new edition, while based primarily upon the content, is also updated, expanded and streamlined, with the facts and information that has further helped entrepreneurs and businesses make sense of the online world. It is expanded in scope, yet simplified in what is critically important to build a strategic online breakthrough that works, with your business.

This is the International Edition, with a new title, cover and new updated content.

www.breakthrough.digital

CONNECTING & TERMINOLOGY

Connecting & Sharing With This Book

If you are reading the hard copy of this book, statistics show that more than likely you are within 50cm of your smart/mobile phone, almost 24 hours a day. It's probably sitting on the desk beside you, in your pocket, or on the armchair. So, take it out; you're going to be using it.

Take a look at some of the links within the pages of the book. These links will direct you to the page, or the specific resources that are being referred to.

You can start here:

www.breakthrough.digital

Want to stay conventional, yet at the same time digital? Take some photos of key elements of the books and some of the quotes and illustrations with your smartphone – then if they give some value to you, share them on your favorite social media network. And if you are so inclined, please feel free to tag me @doylebuehler or #breakthrough so I can thank you personally for the share.

And, if you really feel like sharing, take a selfie with the book and tag me on social media @doylebuehler or Doyle Buehler - I'll be giving out some special training from time to time, for those who do.

Find me on all of the social networks. Please tag me so I can connect and respond to your comments/questions.

Twitter & Instagram: @doylebuehler

Facebook & Linkedin: Doyle Buehler

Email: doyle@dept.digital

www.breakthrough.digital

Terminology

There are some keywords that will be used interchangeably throughout this book. Do you need to know them? Yes, but don't worry, there will not be a test on them at the end of this program. Consider the following perspectives:

1. **Audience:** The group of people that you are marketing to, that can potentially be your customer, or is already your customer. Some people may not necessarily be your target customer, but may still be in your audience. Think of this scenario like a musical conductor - everyone listens, but not everyone will necessarily come for the same reasons.

2. **Customer:** People who are paying or paid for your products or services.

3. **Digital Domain:** No, this is not your website URL. This is everything that you and your business are about, online. It is your entire digital footprint. It is what connects everything to everyone; it is your "inter-tubes". Are you the master of your digital domain? Well, you need to be.

4. **Products:** What you offer as a business. This also includes "services", such as consulting services, professional services, etc. Why classify services as products? Primarily because creating a product from your services provides a much broader aspect of your offering, and allows you to increase your product offering substantially.

5. **Visuals:** The photographs and images that provide references to our visual worlds. Everything that is used, as "collateral" that is part of the overall visual message that we are delivering online.

6. **Channel:** A specific type of media, for example, television. Facebook, Google+, Twitter, etc. are all separate "channels". Your website is also considered a channel. It is important to understand that these channels can work together, but also how they need to create a "micro-habitat" on their own as well, as your audience may only be introduced to you through one specific channel at a time until they get to know you further.

7. **Keywords:** All the words that are specifically related to your business and what you do online. Ideally, you should have a list of 6-10 "key" or significant words that are part of the overriding structure of how you explain to people what your business is about. Ensure you use these words regularly, in all of your content and descriptions, as it begins to build relevance to you and your website.

8. **Digital Platform or Framework:** The overriding structure that encompasses all your digital assets. It is everything you are a part of online, and that is part of your business. This is your strategy, content and all the supporting activities that will be used to build your digital business. Creating your digital platform is the focus of this book.

9. **Business Owners v. Business Leader v. Entrepreneur:** A business owner works "in the business"; business leaders and entrepreneurs have made the transition to be able to work "on the business". They like to use their "Empire Building Brain".

10. **Digital Ecosystem.** All of the parts and pieces of your platform that constitute your ideas, programs, channels, content, social media, web pages, online gifts, etc.

Have other definitions that are not always that clear? Please help me define others for you. Discuss them online.

www.breakthrough.digital

PART 1

#

#

UNDERSTANDING YOUR #BREAKTHROUGH

CHAPTER 1
ARE YOU THE MASTER OF YOUR DIGITAL DOMAIN?

I have traveled the length and breadth of this country and talked with the best people, and I can assure you that data processing is a fad that won't last out the year.

- Prentice Hall editor in charge of business books, 1957

Are You The Master of Your Digital Domain?

Awareness is everything. How do you master your digital "domain"? And no, I don't mean your website domain either - your real online domain consists of every single digital asset that you "own" online. This is your digital ecosystem that you create and build that contains all of your ideas, philosophies and the essence of who you are and the value you deliver - across everything online.

Before creating a proper framework for your business and trying to solve the problems and challenges that you face, you must first understand the actual problems that are encountered online, and then you need to address them. Which ones do you encounter regularly?

Let's get it out of the way. Online is not easy. There are many things that slow us all down. There are many problems that we encounter in our journey to build our perfect business online. Overall, this comes from a misunderstanding of the problems that many businesses encounter. There is no easy solution; first, you need to discover what it is that is going wrong. The online world is really quite ugly and unforgiving.

Where do things start to go "wrong"? Do any of these major problems sound familiar?

The Top 8 Problems That Most Entrepreneurs and Businesses Face Online

1. Too much online apathy with customers. Customers are spending more time, money and resources with your competitors.

2. You have little to no influence online. People are simply not listening or seeing how great and remarkable you actually are.

3. There are never enough leads and committed people. You are unable to develop enough business and contacts to build or sustain your business.

4. No defined or clear strategy for working online exists. Bouncing around from idea to idea happens regularly. Putting out fires is your marketing plan. There is the uncertainty of what exactly to do next.

5. Too much "noise" and clutter online. Too many distractions for your ideal customer to find you and engage with you.

6. Difficulty in finding the "right" customer for your market; the customer who is truly intrigued by what you offer.

7. Confusion with all of the different tools, activities, and types of social media channels. Too many things to consider making any one thing work well. Falling behind in what tools are available for marketing.

8. Thinking that jumping on the next tool, technology or "fad" will save the day (and your business). Social selling? Snapchat? What's the next big shiny thing coming? It won't help you.

Now, it is not always about the biggest problems, but also about the mistakes that we, ourselves make. No, we are not infallible, but we are human. Here's why businesses are not the master of their digital domains:

The Top 9 Mistakes Most Entrepreneurs and Businesses Make Online

1. Not having a proper digital strategy that ties all of your digital assets together, gives your online presence a direction, and delivers your value to your audience.

2. Not knowing what social channels to use and when, and how to integrate social selling. Not understanding how to use social media and the online market space.

3. Forgetting to follow a specific process or methodology for moving online, or developing an online presence and influence.

4. Believing and thinking that your audience online actually cares about who you are or what you do, and will quickly engage and respond to what you have to say.

5. Not having a proper step-by-step plan to tell people about themselves and their company online.

6. Not knowing what tools are easily available to make the process substantially easier.

7. Thinking that everyone already knows about your company and that your information is relevant.

8. Being reactive and unable to provide a clear focus, strategy, and direction to building your online influence.

9. Not understanding that your customer is literally only 1-click away from your competitors, and not delivering your value that keeps them with you.

Are You An Empire Builder?

How do you overcome these mistakes and errors that we all seem to make? Yes, we know online is not easy - if we don't have the right knowledge and the right tools to implement our ideas, they all seem to get lost.

Enter the Empire. Your Online Empire.

Online Empire building is an entrepreneurial philosophy, and the foundation for your business breakthrough. It's about looking at your online strategy – or lack of one – and seeing how you can best leverage online strategies to grow your business, with a solid strategy and plan for implementation.

This is what you can build from the details of this book.

What Exactly Is The Empire Building Mindset & Why Is It Important?

Thinking like an Online Empire Builder will help you get your Breakthrough. It is not some term cooked up to make this whole book and process sound more important than it actually is.

Daniel Priestly, Best-Selling Author and Founder of Dent.Global and Key Person of Influence has developed a unique model that attempts to illustrate the various stages that we all, as entrepreneurs, go through a mental "battle" to get to the level of success that we deem and "feel" is appropriate.

He's eloquently separated our brain into three stages or phases that we need to go through, to get what we want, and to where we want. We try to separate ourselves and get out of entrepreneurial chaos, yet we naturally tend to fall back into these patterns when we are not focused.

We can lose our focus when we feel desperate, when we feel out of control, and where we head mentally when we do not have a proper plan with our business. Where do we start? We start with something that has been with us for millions of years of human evolution, back to our days of lizards and other reptilian beasts. And, even to this day, we quickly revert back to this, the Reptile.

The Reptile is our fear of survival; the fear that what we have, in terms of resources, will be depleted, and depleted quickly. We believe that everyone is there to steal our food, our lunch, and yes, even our business. We are quick to respond unintelligently and fear that we are constantly and consistently losing out. We focus on picturing our severely limiting resources that everyone is seemingly after. We begin to horde and do not reflect on the bigger picture. It is a basic survival mechanism, and it is there for a reason - to help us survive. As an entrepreneur, you need to do more than just survive.

WHAT BRAIN ARE YOU BUILDING?

Our Reptilian Response; it is not part of our truly intellectual brain. It is our fight or flight response; one that may get us the short-term goals, but consistently jeopardizes our long-term futures. It is the "Get Rich Quick," "Make 6 or 7 figures," or even better, "make money while you sleep" of the online domain. It is our immediate response to most things; we are prone to make bad decisions for the most part, as a result of this immediate response.

The tragic thing is that it is an automatic response; you can, however, learn to overcome this - if you can focus on the bigger side of things, the bigger picture of things; your overall strategy. This is where your thought processes need to be re-wired towards your ultimate goal, your ultimate focus of empire building. Understanding it, and acknowledging it for what it is will be the only mechanisms that enable you to overcome this behavior.

You can pick out these behaviors, as well as pick out the people that are exhibiting these behaviors. What does this look like? We'll see it in simple concepts like affiliate marketing through "multiple streams of income", the "one-big-win" scenario, "make money online," the concept of "passive income," "getting huge traffic to your site", and of course my all-time favorite, "Make 6 figures" (without even trying), ad infinitum. The online world is full of these, and like most of us, we have all fallen for its charm of getting rich, creating immense traffic online, or having an immense email list where everyone supposedly responds quickly to...."And, all in 2 easy payments of $47! But wait, there is more..."

The problem is that these so-called solutions are always short-lived, if it actually works; it is never a long-term strategy; it is used for that instantaneous response that triggers that need; that demonstration that everything is limited, and that we will miss out. It is, in fact, the fear of missing out.

This is why we all buy crap online that we never actually use. I know - I have spent oodles on tools, programs and software that I have never ever used. Someone made some money, but it certainly wasn't me or many other eager businesses.

While it can be effective at times (and, mostly for the one who is selling this to you), it leaves most of us feeling emptied and somewhat cheapened by the experience.

Doyle Buehler

So, where does our brain head next, once we have overcome this reptilian response, with limited resource thinking, and the belief that we don't know where our next lunch is coming from? Yes, monkeys.

Our monkey brain is, in essence, the focus of the bright and shiny objects all around us. It is about our familiarity with things, our own comfort. It is about "bright and shiny objects" - seemingly chasing our tails as we look for the next thing that will bring our success, the next thing that will help build our business. And yes, it is drama, and it also is Facebook.

All of the new tools and new social media channels are all part of the problem, and they focus exactly on your monkey brain – how to drop everything for the possibility that it just might work better. In most cases it doesn't – we've simply wasted more time and more money discovering that this is not that answer.

It's also about us thinking that "busy" is something good and that we all should just be busy, as something will get done. We really need to stop the glorification of "busy"; the actions are typically futile, as they have no real connection to where we truly want to go and how we are going to get there. We've all heard of the expression about a room full of monkeys with typewriters will (eventually) be able to type a novel.

Our monkey brain is primarily activity-based. It's our attempt to try to get stuff done, without much actually happening. It is us working in the hamster-wheel. How can we make ourselves "look" busy? That's our monkey brain talking.

Overcoming these various stages of your brain are extremely instrumental in our success of our business. How do we overcome them, and get to the Empire Builder, as part of your personality and better yet, behaviors with your business for a breakthrough? You need to readjust how you think and how you problem solve. You need to build a strong strategy for your business; you need to remove the self-perpetuating distractions, you need to work on your business, not in your business. This is how you change things.

We may think that we are "above all this", but sadly we are not. Take a look at your business, and you will quickly see whether or not what you think is what you are doing. One of the key identifiers is quite simple - do you have a digital or online business strategy? Do you actually know what your brand "essence" is about? Do you find yourself putting out fires? Do you feel overwhelmed by the information that is out there, and what you should do, could do, maybe need to do? When someone asks, "how are you doing", your typical response is "busy". This is your evolutionary brain not doing what it is supposed to be doing. The good news? Most business leaders all do this, and usually unaware of it. The powerful thing is that you can overcome this; you can focus on what is more important to your and your business.

Memes and viral marketing? These are both accurate understandings of our monkey brain. We all know what they are - memes are those stupid yet funny cat videos and photos, the picture that you see circulated time and time again. They are "bright and shiny"; they are a distraction, and yes, they are hardly ever repeatable. They are brief in experience. We all like shiny things; amazingly, so do monkeys.

How do we get past the reptile response and the monkey brain? What is next?

This is the domain where real business leaders are. This is the point of your Online Empire thinking, this is the point of creating the Breakthrough for your business. This is the mindset of Digital Leadership. This is where the real changes take place. This is where the real entrepreneurs and the real leaders come forth. This is not just a place, but rather it is a way of thinking. Consider it the true meaning of entrepreneurship; how we actually think about things is as important as how we do things. This is where this can actually happen.

It's not a magical, mysterious place habited by wizards and magicians or even hypnotists. It's a place where we can unleash our true intuition, where we can trust, honor and respect everyone in our circles, and outside. It is where we can actually create the influence that really matters.

This is the Empire Builder part of your brain. The part that embraces the changes, the part that actually relays it in a concept that is always constructive and always available. It is a state of mind, where all resources are there, for you to take maximum advantage of. It is the way of thinking that your resources are available somewhere and somehow - you just need to actually find them, engage them and enable them. Your resources are in fact everywhere, and abundantly available. You just need to build the guidance towards them.

In this Empire Building mindset, you can leave behind the monkey and reptile brains and focus on your key tasks at hand. And no, it is not our tactic of marketing to appeal to your reptile brain or monkey brain, either (although that can give you extra marketing points, but that is another book into itself, and would in fact prove my point).

How do you actually embrace this so-called 'Empire Builder' of digital leadership? Imagine if you had unlimited resources, unlimited money, unlimited partners to help you. This is how you get started in Empire Building. The way that you think is plentiful. You will attract high performing people, and you will be able to get the job done.

The Business Breakthrough, as part of this book, is what I have created in order to allow you to focus on what is important, and get rid of everything that is not. It allows you to build a sound strategy, and create an activity plan that keeps you on task. The strategic architecture that you will create as part of this framework helps keep your business from wandering from project to project, and from social channel to social channel. It helps you define the purpose of you and your business in an easy to understand format. It kicks you in the ass! It tells you that you can shut down that reptile response and the monkey moments; and gets you to lay the proper framework for your online empire, like a true entrepreneur.

This framework helps you get rid of all of the distractions and keeps the overwhelming feelings from overtaking you and what you do. You can use it to jump start your business, as well as keep you on course. It all starts with your strategy that works in the online world.

How to discover if you have a reptilian brain or a monkey brain, or better yet, an Empire Building brain? Ask yourself some simple questions:

1.   Have you ever bought an online tool to help you build traffic?

2.   Have you ever "dabbled" in money-making affiliate marketing?

3.   Have you ever "perked up" when you encounter a supposedly "newer" opportunity?

4.   How many "big ideas" do you have going on at any moment?

5.   How many times have you clicked on that "make money from home" ad?

6.   How many ab-blasters, slap-chops and useless kitchen utensils do you own?

Did You Know That You Might be Missing Out on 67% of Your Sales?

Despite what you actually do accomplish online, we are still missing a few of the most critical pieces to building a breakthrough online. Simply put, most of your perfect, ideal clients are not looking for you. Even though they need you desperately. They simply don't know that you exist. Or, even worse, they know that you exist, but are not sure exactly what you can do for them.

And further, not everyone is, in fact, your customer, nor will ever become your customer! So, why are you wasting money looking for these people who don't care about you or what you have to offer?

Let's explore this idea and figure out how to remedy it!

How does this breakdown?

The people that are perfect, ideal clients for you can generally be broken down into the following percentages:

1.   3% Ready to buy

2.   7% Open to you

3.   30% Never will buy from you

4.   30% Not aware that you are there

5.   30% Aware that they have a problem, but not sure how to solve it.

Everyone becomes short-sighted online. We focus on the 3% when our biggest market are those that we need to educate and inform, to get them into the buying space. We need to nurture our audience towards the goal of a sale, lead, referral, or whatever metric is critical to your business.

ARE YOU MISSING 67% OF YOUR MARKET?

Not Everyone Is Ready To Buy From You Right Now

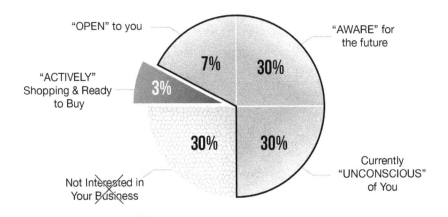

Nurture Your Audience Over Time To Progress Them Through Their Buyers Process

Sadly, most online businesses fail to utilize this. And, while it is more predominant in a non-ecommerce site, most sites feel sufficient to have a simple "contact us" page on their website, expecting people to contact you. Not very pro-active, is it?

The 3% is actually a very small number, right? What would happen if you were able to nudge people into this final purchasing position, quicker than normal? Or even better, educate them on a solution, and build the relationship, before they are able to make the decision.

So, how do you make the additional 67% actively work towards sales? You need to nurture them along the buyer's cycles. You need to actively engage them with "education" and "community" through your expertise and knowledge, to move them towards their ultimate purchase with you.

This is why you must have a clear and congruent digital strategy, which ties everything together. Otherwise, your audience will only see your noise and your confusion across everything.

The Online Empire Project allows your business to extend this buying relationship into the full 67% of your entire audience that can and will purchase at some point. You are building the infrastructure necessary to be able to capitalize on this, with what you will learn.

This is the focus of a solid digital strategy – to encompass all of these possibilities. This is what customer nurturing is all about.

There Are No Awards For Second Best. Are You Tired of Mediocrity Online?

We all talk about having a better business online. Seldom do we seek the knowledge and expertise that can actually get us there. Are you ready to move past mediocrity, to get to exactly where you want to be? Do you really want to be in the driver's seat and get shit done? You can get there if you focus on a simple solution to building a solid platform for your business wanting more out of online - more people, more profile, and more profit.

So, how will you get there? By doing amazing and remarkable things, that's how. Getting shit done, as they say.

The Digital "Pledge"

Before getting further into this book, I want you to make a commitment – not to me – to yourself.

You've decided to read this book because your want to improve your online business or the online aspect of your business. You've decided that you want to create a breakthrough online.

So, before we begin, please raise your right hand and repeat after me:

I will take control of my own business online.

No one knows my business better than myself.

I refuse to be misled by the industry.

I am taking charge of my own business, in my own industry.

I will concentrate on what is important, and disregard the misinformation that is prevalent.

I will become the leader in my industry. I will surpass my competitors.

I will no longer be deluded by what others say and cause me to think about online.

I will become the master of my own digital domain.

I will build my online empire.

I will create #breakthrough with my business.

Let's get moving!

THE DIGITAL LEADERSHIP **MANIFESTO**

THERE HAS NEVER BEEN A BETTER TIME TO OWN YOUR **FUTURE** ONLINE WITH YOUR BUSINESS. **THE SUCCESS** OF YOU AND YOUR BUSINESS IS ONLY ABOUT **BUILDING** YOUR KNOWLEDGE BASE, USING THE TOOLS THAT YOU HAVE, AND **BEING SMART** ABOUT WHAT YOU DO AND HOW **YOU DO IT.**

STOP WASTING TIME, MONEY AND RESOURCES ON SOLUTIONS THAT DON'T PROVIDE A CLEAR VISION, A CLEAR STRATEGY, AND MORE IMPORTANTLY, A KEY WAY TO IMPLEMENT WHAT YOU HAVE LEARNED.

BECOME THE MASTER OF YOUR DIGITAL DOMAIN. **NOW IS THE TIME TO BECOME THE DIGITAL LEADER THE AUTHORITY IN YOUR NICHE.**

NOW IS THE TIME TO BECOME THE DIGITAL LEADER IN YOUR **BUSINESS**

STOP THE SELF-PERPETUATION OF THE THINGS THAT ARE **WRONG** WITH THE ONLINE WORLD. REFUSE TO BE SEGREGATED OR PREACHED TO.

NOW IS THE TIME TO **CREATE YOUR #BREAKTHROUGH**

Breakthrough.Digital

CHAPTER 2
THE 7 DEADLY DIGITAL DELUSIONS

"

I think there is a world market for maybe 5 computers. *"*

**- Thomas Watson,
IBM CEO, 1943**

The 7 Deadly Digital Delusions

Many businesses do not actually realize what pieces are missing, and how critical it is to understand what they need to do, how, and when. When to use Facebook, when not to; why to use SEO, what about content? Entrepreneurs are really feeling STUCK and overwhelmed.

And, the really ugly part - we are being misled and misinformed about a lot of different things online. There is a tremendous amount of confusion here, which is caused by the industry itself; it is caused by the interests of the various business types within the online industry - the social media businesses, the SEO agencies, the advertising agencies, the web developers, the graphic designers. Each group has subsequently created these silos, which have actually negatively affected how we build businesses online.

We've moved away from congruency across our digital ecosystems; and relied on individual silos that are not able to actually connect everything, strategically nor practically. Everyone wants a piece of the action, and so will only handle one specific area, without the knowledge and understanding of how all of these pieces fit together, to create congruency.

This needs to be changed, today, by you.

Businesses are suffering and in a lot of cases, closing their doors online because of the scale of these problems. It is all very painful. Sound familiar?

I found the base of these problems to be specific patterns of behaviors and knowledge that were really incongruent with what was actually going on.

The digital delusions highlight these challenges, assumptions, attitudes, behaviors, pains and problems that we are all encountering as we try to grow our business online.

Why delusions? Why not 'Myths'? A delusion is an actual way of thinking – it is based upon our own inherent assumptions and biases that we hold towards the industry. Whether we like it or not, our mind seems to be wired for specific behaviours, despite knowledge to the contrary. No, we are not stupid, either - we simply have been 'forced' to think this way as a result of the quick growth of online and the internet. It is what is 'expected'. Look at any ecosystem that grows quickly - it is usually a weed.

We need to get rid of all of the weeds.

We need to get rid of all of the assumptions and biases.

We need to change the way that we think online.

Preventing You From Creating Your #Breakthrough

After many years of asking the questions that were important to business leaders and entrepreneurs, as well as my own experience in the field, all the misbeliefs, misconceptions, and misunderstandings were collated to form what I've called the 7 Deadly Digital Delusions. These are the delusions that are most likely directly affecting your business and your business success online - the ones directly preventing you from building your online empire. They are:

1.   Guru-speak and buzz words get results.

2. Social Media is a strategy.

3. Online works in isolation.

4. Advertising is dead and ineffective online.

5. I don't need a "sales funnel" sales will come in time.

6. Being online is "easy", just write about a successful story.

7. Customers will always be able to find me, or, "Build it, and they will come".

In this book, we further reinforce what you and your business need to accomplish to actually fully overcome these delusions, by building up your online business through the unique digital framework.

Deadly Digital Delusion #1

| 1 | Guru-speak and buzz words get results |

What Is The Delusion?

The word "guru" is highly misused in this industry. In most industries or areas of expertise, it is actually a highlight of their skills and advancement to a higher level of knowledge and capabilities. In this industry however, anyone can call themselves a guru, even from working in their basement, with little or no qualifications whatsoever, further adding fuel to the fire for creating this huge chasm of misinformation. No, we don't all need Masters degrees to market a business, but we do need a baseline.

"Gurus" in this industry will not save your business. Only you can do that.

This is one of the fundamental delusions that everyone is subjected to. Whether it is because the majority of people don't actually understand everything that is going on, or just that there are a lot of people trying to drive into this space to become the "expert"; either can be debated, but it is, in fact, a combination of both.

The amount of knowledge and information that you are expected to know about being online really is immense, and in most cases, simply overwhelming. Most businesses just want to focus on their business, not on the seemingly superfluous stuff like online marketing.

It is not a sign of laziness or lack of focus either, but rather a symptom of the level of detail required to get started and stay up to date with all aspects and also implement on a regular basis. Most people will simply decide that it is not worth the trouble, and just let things fade away, hoping that it will get better "by design".

We are inundated with so much information and an array of different aspects to keep up, that it can be overwhelming for most.

From the "guru" side, many people who think that they are "entrepreneurs" feel that building up a "social media company" is quick and easy, and there will be lots of customers. It is like that old gold-rush model that doesn't really work anymore. Everyone and their dog are considered a social media expert these days.

The problem is not so much that more people are entering the online space, just that there is no certification, no regulation, no formal training required to get into this space. Often, the knowledge level of the so-called "experts" providing the advice is sometimes questionable and usually generated by simply surfing the web for good material. There are really very few people who can actually understand the needs of the clients aligned with the actual needs of the business.

With the volume of information always coming in, it is easier to get someone else to do the work for them. This will help you and your business, but the strategy of the actual business needs to be understood quite clearly. It needs to be clear how the different pieces fit together for your business. Every business is unique, and it does take particular skills to be able to understand and comprehend what needs to be done for an individual business and also how it needs to be done. You need to be able to understand what is needed, to be able to select and utilize these various services, to discover the path you need to take. You need to be able to screen people properly, to ensure that they fit with your overall messages and strategies that are at the root of your success.

If you are unable to complete the online development on your own, you need to source and utilize known experts in the field; people whose work you have seen directly, or those who come highly recommended. It is far too easy for anyone to put up a sign and say that they are open for business as a social media expert. Worse yet, say they are part of your "target" demographic, and hence assume that they can then handle everything else, just because they are "smart about social media". It takes much, much more than this.

Anyone can sit at their computer and be a self-proclaimed Facebook expert or guru. It takes some essential business and marketing skills to be able to actually connect what is known with what is not known, and at the same time, interface and integrate what your company is specifically about and how the message is being conveyed. It's not easy being able to do this.

It's about connecting the business side of things to the online side of things that really can grow your business.

Overcoming The Delusion

You would be surprised about how much you know that actually affects what you do and can do online. Online strategies come down to the essence of your business, which can be conveyed well by the business leader. Working online needs to be a close part of what you do, every day, and needs to be integrated into everything that you do for your business. You still need to be the expert; the expert in your business. No one can do that except you.

While there are principles of online work that are similar in structure, your business is unique, and the approach that you need to take in developing a strategy will also be unique. You need to be able to combine the essence of your business with an online methodology that takes into account your distinctive business.

If you are doing the work internally, the same rules apply; you really need to get the best person for the job. They need to have the skills of strategic sensibilities, technical knowledge, and excellent means of communication.

In sourcing external assistance for your online business, you need to do some digging when you hire someone to complete this type of role. It is key to your business and should be treated as such.

A digital media consultant is essentially the eyes, ears, and voice of your company online. That means you need someone who can raise your brand awareness, deliver your audience to your website (not just traffic), and boost your bottom line, all while keeping your company's reputation top-of-mind.

You need to ask and engage the person or firm fully. Don't be afraid to ask key questions that will truly point you in the direction of whether or not this person or company is for you and will help your company. You need to assess how they problem solve, and how they actually create unique strategies that will work for your business, not just off-the-shelf solutions that have been thrown in place for multiple, previous clients. It's no different than what you would do when you are interviewing someone for a job. You need to know exactly who you are getting and what they are capable of, otherwise, you wouldn't hire them. You need the best people to do the best for your business.

Having said this, keep in mind that you, in fact, are the "expert"; no one knows your business better than you do. It is, therefore, important to ensure that you fully complete the analysis as to what you need to do, in the online space. Become accountable for your business.

Reflection/Action

Here are some questions you can ask when selecting people to work with. Asking these questions will help you to quickly get to understand whether or not the person or company is suitable for what you want to accomplish.

1. How successful are you in your own digital space?

2. Do you understand my market?

3. How connected are you to influencers in my industry?

4. What tools do you use to measure the ROI of your campaigns?

5. What are some social media campaign ideas for my business?

6. How would you handle a social media crisis?

Deadly Digital Delusion #2

2 | **Social Media and Facebook are strategies**

What Is The Delusion?

Many companies and individuals feel that being on social media is all that is needed to be successful online. That, if they have a Facebook page, for example, their business is "good to go".

Facebook is a tool.

Social Media is a tool.

Are there successful businesses that use only Facebook? Yes, but these are in fact quite rare. Typically, successful businesses work across all of the different channels and have implemented an integrated online strategy with all of the different components. Social media is only a fragment of your entire digital ecosystem.

There is much more to an online business than one social media element. As we established, it is important to integrate all the different activities and strategies to make a business work better.

You need to ask yourself: how does a Facebook page fit into your strategy? How does a Facebook customer fit into your sales funnel? How do they make connections with your business?

Overcoming The Delusion

Entrepreneurs that recognize that social media is part of an online strategy can recognize precisely how to use each tool, and how each tool works in conjunction with other online tools that are available to each and every business.

Having said this, there is no real magic about social media either. As we explored in some of our online trends, it really is more about connecting what we enjoy. It is about being social.

Think of social media and all of the social channels as being part of your online business toolkit. You need to know what tool to use and when. There are so many different tools available that you need to be able to understand which tools best fit with your business and of course your audience. Are you a B2B or a B2C? Do you deal with "fun" type of content, sales-based, or do you work better with factual, engineering based information? These are aspects that you will need to consider in choosing what social media tools you need.

Reflection/Action

You need to decide what is important to you and your business in assessing the channels of social media. Making a list and combining aspects of your customers and audience, in terms of where they are located, or visiting, helps you work out what is important and needs to be done.

Consider the following:

1.   What channels are you currently using?

2.   What channels have you considered using?

3.   What channels do you feel that you must use? Why?

4.   Where is your audience currently migrating? What are they using? Where are they most active? Do you have evidence of this?

Deadly Digital Delusion #3

 **3 | Online works in isolation**

What Is The Delusion?

Many businesses believe that what they do online is separate from what they do in their "normal" offline state. They feel that there needs to be a segregation that allows them to compartmentalize what happens within each part of their business. Further, a significant misunderstanding is that they only have to work on one specific component and are still able to get maximum results.

Businesses that are usually effective online have already built a very strong business in their regular bricks and mortar world. Are you connecting people offline with your online business, and are you connecting your online community with your offline business?

The interconnection is more than just putting a Twitter handle on your business card. You need to think holistically how the two separate parts are integrated throughout. You need to integrate everything that happens in both worlds.

Think of the Internet as being the umbilical cord that connects each "side" of your business. It connects, and more importantly, allows for your audience to reach you wherever you are, and wherever they are.

Overcoming The Delusion

Fundamentally, the objective is to have both your online and offline business working in unison. If you have an existing physical location, you need to consider how to transition customers from your physical store or office locations, towards your online activities. If you choose to have a physical location, then you can easily ensure and leverage the capabilities towards compelling people online, and vice versa, whereby you can direct your online traffic through to your actual location.

You need to look at ways that you can connect your online audience with your offline store/shop or business. You can do this with such things as location redemption coupons that are displayed online, or special offers that are only accepted offline.

From your physical location, you need to engage people with such things as photo check-ins, location check-ins, or special offers and discounts to your online presence. This can also be accomplished with such things as special events where the goals and objectives are to specifically get customers or clients to move from your physical location onto your online store/shop. One of the important things to consider is properly incentivising this move from offline to online domains.

You need to engage your audience into your overall sales funnel. This then allows you to approach them at different stages of your engagement and subsequent buying cycle. The businesses that can engage their audience in either domain and provide a smooth transition between the two, are the ones that will survive and become very successful. This concept will be explored further in the Breakthrough Strategy.

Reflection/Action

To get a better idea of how your business is structured, consider the following questions:

1. Do you have an existing physical or retail location?

2. What elements of a comprehensive digital strategy do you use? SEO? Advertising? Social Media? Content Planning?

3. How can you connect your online audience with your offline activities?

4. How can you drive your audience online, from your physical locations? How do you incentivise this transaction?

Deadly Digital Delusion #4

4 | Advertising is dead and ineffective online

What Is The Delusion?

Many businesses don't believe that advertising works online – that they can't actually connect properly with their audience, that it is too hard, and, that you must spend thousands and thousands of dollars to get results, like the "big boys". Having a website and a Facebook page should be enough, right?

Surely advertising must be dead? What, with all the talk of "social" media, "social" selling?

Throw enough money at it, and surely it should work?

Sadly, many businesses have done just that - spent thousands and thousands of dollars. Without ANY results. Thus the belief soon becomes that advertising will not work. There are thousands upon thousands of businesses who have tried and failed at online advertising, perpetuating the belief, or delusion that it doesn't work.

Even the big businesses are guilty of this. Budgets of $100k+ per month that get little results, so they simply try to throw more money at it, in the hopes of getting some result. It doesn't work either.

It seems like all advertising is not working.

The problem seems to be more endemic.

As businesses owners, we feel that we don't get the results that we "should", yet we are prone to using our bad experience with the results when it simply is a problem of not knowing quite what we need to know.

This delusion seems to also come from traditional forms of advertising (read: old school), when you would advertise in the Yellow Pages, and have a stream of calls coming in for your business. Sadly, the reason why the Yellow Pages is (mostly) defunct is the same reason that most businesses fail at advertising today - we are using dated marketing techniques with dated information.

It used to be about "eyeballs" - get as many people to look at what you have, and surely some people will become customers. Despite what Yellow Pages or display ads tell you, neither of these work.

It actually still amazes me that this delusion is further exacerbated by the industry itself, in the desire to get you to spend more, with little understanding of the 'why' of you and your business.

Overcoming The Delusion

Advertising still lives on.

Yes, many people use ad blockers and have tuned out of banner ads, but many techniques can work if set up properly.

It's no different than expanding your circle of influence. Social media and your website content will only get you so far; then it becomes a problem of exposure.

The problem, however, is not so much that advertising is dead, but rather we have gotten away from results as well as your specific audience. We need to focus on the results, as well as, and more importantly, your audience.

Most campaigns are designed around a simple "fact" - get the demographic right and you will have your target audience. Male or female? 18-25? What is their postal code? If you have this information, then everything will be ok. Wrong.

While we can believe that this is the pathway, we couldn't be further from the real truth, those demographics are in fact limiting who you target.

We will never be entirely "rid" of it. It is integrated into society, so get used to it. It will eventually come to all social networking services, as the services themselves also need to generate revenue. You can, however, leverage it and change how you use it to actually make it successfully work for your particular business. There is a specific way to capture leads, sales, downloads, etc., and that way is integrating all of the different activities across your business.

Find out exactly who your customer is - get more into the 'why'. Why they buy, how they behave, where they hang out, what they do with their spare time. Take a look at the complete picture of who exactly is your perfect customer.

This is what is called owning your niche. Find out exactly who is enabled by what you have, and you have niched. Target these people only. The simple fact is that not everyone even wants to be your customer. So why would you waste money sending them ads? The realization that "everybody" is not your market is one of the first steps you can take to growing your business.

By isolating your customer, you can then have a direct conversation with them. What you are saying becomes more relevant, if your customer knows implicitly that you are talking to them. It is no different than your responses to ads and promotion - you only are interested in what interests you. You simply ignore the rest.

In developing an ad platform, think about your entire digital ecosystem. Traditional banner and interruption ads will decline, however, and will be replaced by innovative offerings like Promoted Tweets and Sponsored Stories. What makes these so-called native ads unique is that they don't look like ads at all apart from small disclaimers. They appear in-stream and read exactly like another piece of user-generated content.

While some users resent this intrusion into their home streams, these "native" ads potentially enable brands to reach clients on their own turf and on their own terms. Behind it all, is the concept of convergence; the idea that ads and content can be interchangeable. Companies, for instance, are already sending out Tweets to followers on their social media channels. Using analytical tools to identify which are most read, they can selectively amplify the best of the bunch as Promoted Tweets, turning content into ads and reaching an even larger audience.

It is important to look at advertising with a different perspective. Facebook and Linkedin have begun to move or transition the types of advertising that most people will respond to. You no longer need to have some general type ad that you hope your specific target audience may chance upon. It is no longer about getting just eyeballs on your ads – it's about making sure that your ads reach your target audience. There is no longer any second-guessing; you need to focus your advertising on specific interests, activities, passions, plus, of course, the regular demographics that you are used to such as age, occupation, gender, etc.

Facebook has actually moved several steps forward recently, and will no doubt continue to evolve their advertising methods. Facebook has introduced some ways to connect through ads that allow you to engage with people in the Facebook network who may share similar interests. This allows you to share more information. You now have a tremendous amount of flexibility and capabilities, where you can directly target extremely specific audiences.

This book is obviously not about advertising, as that is a complete, complex subject unto itself. It is important though to understand some of the basics of advertising and in particular, the channels that are available to you and your business, in an online perspective, and how they can work directly for you.

We won't be able to discuss traditional media advertising; this is important on a case by case basis. It should be implemented at some point. However, like online advertising, extremely specific goals and target audiences need to be set to work properly with your business.

Reflection/Action

Advertising is a sound strategy for creating brand awareness as well as generating sales and leads. Without advertising of some form, whether it is through Google Adwords, Facebook ads, mobile advertising, social network ads/posts, or even traditional media advertising – you will not increase your audience and sales.

Online advertising needs to be an ongoing activity - whether it is on Facebook, Twitter, Instagram, Linkedin, Google, or whatever other channel is appropriate to you and your business, because not all forms of online advertising are "equal", especially from the perspective of aligning with your own business strategy.

You need to be very clear about your objectives - whether you are "brand building", or looking for specific sales - only then can campaigns that work specifically for you and your business be designed.

And, you must focus directly on your own perfect customer. This is the only way that your ads will really connect, and result in sales.

Now ask yourself these specific questions:

1. Who is your target audience? What do they like? Where do they go? What do they talk about? How can you identify them online?

2. What is your goal of advertising? Make it specific - do customers need to download something?

3. How does it fit with your sales funnel? How are you moving people towards your product/service?

4. What specifically are you actually trying to communicate with your audience?

5. What is special and unique about what you have to offer or your advertisement?

6. What is your ROI and your daily spend on advertising?

7. What channel does your audience best represent?

Deadly Digital Delusion #5

I don't need a "sales funnel" for ROI. Sales will come in time.

What Is The Delusion?

Businesses can lose the plot amidst the clutter and confusion of online – they can become so focused on developing an online strategy that they forget what their purpose is. Other businesses manage to maintain focus but have no goal for moving observers into leads, buyers or contacts. They simply have a website with a "Contact Us" page.

Ask yourself the question - how many times have you used a "contact us" page and filled out the form? Possibly a few, but again, you are no different than most of your customers. The "contact us" page is for those people who typically are ready to buy, which equates to about 3% of all of your site visitors. What about the rest of them?

You are in common company - very few sites have a sales funnel - which is the progressive nurturing of a lead into an actual sale. If you miss the 3% that don't actually buy nor fill out your contact us page, then what? You've lost the sale.

There are also many businesses using Facebook who seem to be just using it as a community-based forum of yesteryear. There is no push towards their e-commerce site and no mention of products that customers can buy. There simply is a collection of "nice" & "funny"... and of course cats and bacon. This does not create business; this does not inform and educate; it does not move the audience towards an eventual purchase, or even onto an email list.

This is ineffective online marketing at its finest, and something that you must avoid.

Overcoming The Delusion

The broad goal is obviously to increase or sustain revenues. The more specific goals need to be exactly what you want your audience to do. No business will grow without paying customers - even if you are a not-for-profit business, you still need to generate income to grow the business or increase your impact.

If you operate a commerce-based site, then obviously the final action is a purchase. If you are running something less tangible, you still need to consider how to capture your audience. Even if your final action is just to inform, your site needs to be able to "capture" this step, with such things as a download, a gift, an email, entry into a contest, or something similar. When you are formulating your strategy, ensure that you understand this process and can add "goals" along the way.

Sales funnels do not necessarily imply only for a specific dollar value or "sales". A sales funnel is necessary in order to guide your audience to a conclusion or specific "action".

This is nurturing. Nurturing your customer to a sales outcome.

Ths action can be as simple as the download of an ebook, or the completion of a form, but something needs to be in place. Sales cycles can be short or long, and it is critical that you capture your audience throughout the entire sales or activity cycle.

If you are unfamiliar with a sales funnel, it is important to understand what one is.

A sales funnel is all of the activities related to what you do, as a business, which drives your user or audience towards a specific goal or action. The action can be as detailed as making a purchase or entering an email address into a sales list. You need to be able to quickly identify what it is that you are driving your audience towards, formulate that as a goal, and then push your traffic and audience towards it.

A sales funnel can be fairly easy to implement. What it means, in essence, is that you have a specific goal, and a means for moving your audience and customers along the steps to reach that goal.

You should consider having multiple goals as well, to fully take advantage of the behaviors surrounding each of your buying stages. This will allow your audience to be able to connect with you along different stages of the buying cycle

Every activity along the way needs to direct your audience to that goal. It can be anything that is related to your business, including:

• An eBook download

• Online store purchase

• Email sign-up for a newsletter

• Contact your business for further information

• White Paper Download

• Checklist or information to read

• Call your CSR line for information

• Download a "gift"

Keep in mind that it is not necessarily an end goal either - it is a step along your process to your core business.

Here is how you can establish an easy to run sales funnel for your business:

1. Set up your analytics package to include goals and other actions.

2. Always ensure there is some takeaway for your audience, at some point in the sales cycle.

3. Utilize links towards your ultimate goal, throughout all sales cycles, all channels, and all of your online and offline activities; push your audience towards your goals throughout all of these different aspects of their journey with you.

Reflection/Action

Consider these questions in analyzing your sales funnel:

1. What are the top 3 goals that you want your audience to "take-away"?

2. What does your sales funnel look like?

3. How will you connect these goals to your actual website?

4. When will you implement and automate your revised sales funnel?

5. How will you monitor and engage your audience with your sales funnel?

Deadly Digital Delusion #6

6 | Online is "easy". Just write about a good story.

What Is The Delusion?

"All I need to do is put up a website, and it will be like opening up a new bank account that is never empty" - wrong. One of the biggest delusions is that the web is somehow some magical rags to riches type scenario. The ongoing and never-ending gold rush of the 21st century. The Internet is just awash apparently in money to be made for everyone.

You have probably seen those dreadful ads, where unscrupulous businesses are touting, "as a mom, I just made $13,421 online, and now I can show you how".

Are you tired of the persistent ads for "Build your 6 or 7 figure business overnight!"? I am.

Even if you have a "legitimate" business, you need to be aware that the journey of taking it from your idea to an online empire is going to take time, it is going to take resources, and it is going to take money.

For some reason, and perhaps because of the "Internet riches" and "overnight success" mentality, a lot of businesses believe that it is a very easy task to do and that once your business is set up, it just is a matter of letting it run on autopilot. Nothing could be further from the truth.

The Internet has always been spoken of as the greatest opportunity our generation has ever seen. The reality is slightly different though, as many are not actually taking full advantage of it. A typical business will usually spend only around 10% of its time and resources on its online component. And it's not always because they don't want to spend – many companies are not focusing on the online domain of their business because they simply do not understand what they 'should' be doing online.

Can you imagine how big your business could become if you dedicated even a few more resources to online activities? Improving your online operations can gain you a huge competitive advantage – there's a huge chasm between what is available online and how many businesses are actually exploiting it.

Overcoming The Delusion

Whether you do the online work yourself, or assign the activities, being successful online takes work and dedication.

Invest 20% of your total resources into online, and you will start to chip away at success. You will get there. Anything less and you will not become remarkable, nor exhibit influence online for your audience. What happens if you don't? Your competitors will.

Remember, you're only 1-click away from your competitors and a lost sale or opportunity.

While you need to tell your story, you also actually need to "work it". Your story is important, but it is the implementation that makes the difference. Many businesses talk about blogging, yet never actually do it. You need to have a clear content schedule that allows you to prioritize all your content, ideas and topics. Then you need to get down to business and actually put it in action. Then, either assign the task or assign the goal to get it done.

Consider activities such as blogging as core to your business. It is as important as having sales people on the floor of your traditional store, as it affects your influence in so many ways online. You also need to ensure that you complement all of your online activity together, including press releases, cross promoting your feeds, all with the ultimate goal of building your community and audience online.

Reflection/Action

Here is what you can do, to work 'on' your business:

1. Dedicate 20-30% of your time as a minimum to the online domain of your business. This includes daily writing and developing your sales funnel.

2. Understand and schedule your daily activities based on your online activities as a priority.

3. Consider how you will schedule your staff towards alignment of your strategy and your business' daily working activities.

4. What key tasks need to be accomplished by you and your staff to "work" your business?

5. What new goals can you set towards building your online empire, regarding budgets, staff resources?

Deadly Digital Delusion #7

What Is The Delusion?

We have all heard the expression - build it, and they will come.

In the "old" days, you could set up a shop in your local town or city, put up a sign, and stock your shelves. People would be able to find you, as the journey was not usually that complicated, and your business was typically the only one, or one of a few out there. That scenario no longer exists. With the global market that is now opened up in front of you through the net, the level of competitors has increased, and at the same or a greater level of your own business. Today, you simply will not stand out amongst the clutter online; it is just too big to overcome on your own.

The Internet is a never-ending "web" of connections and terms, images and files. There are 571 websites created online every single minute of every day, and 48 hours of video are uploaded to YouTube in the same amount of time. If you are not doing the right things at the right time, no one will find you.

Many businesses believe in the so-called "magic pill": Search Engine Optimisation (SEO). Unfortunately, this is a very difficult area to work in. Many SEO Professionals will try to sell you a strategy that is designed to "Get you listed as #1 on Google" – sounds great – but this approach to SEO is very one-dimensional, and doesn't take into consideration all of the cornerstones of a complete and sound online strategy.

It is not just about SEO. Everything you do online can be searched, and indexed by the search engines - not just the text of your website, but also the images, photos, videos, and any other type of media that you can imagine. There are a number of activities that need to be integrated across your new online empire strategy that will make it easier to get found online. Without them, and without a sound strategy, you will simply not be found online, other than from friends and family, and maybe only if they feel sorry for you.

Another part of this delusion is the belief in viral marketing. "Going viral" is not a strategy. In fact, trying to "go viral" is similar to buying a lottery ticket – good luck!

Overcoming The Delusion

Instant traffic generators do not exist. While it is easy to just "run some ads" to build traffic, you also have to have a sound foundation to be able to manage and actually utilize the online advertising that you do use. Further, while Google and the other search engines will eventually find you, this will take some time and effort on your part.

There is significant amount of involvement and engagement that must happen for you to build your audience and community. Building a website or putting together a Facebook fan page, will not generate traffic into your sales funnel unless you take an active role in it.

The Business Breakthrough is based more on "Organic" SEO, meaning SEO that you can build naturally into your complete online presence. This means simple things like always fully describing you and your business in every channel that you operate in, writing PR across the Internet, blogging at least once a week, changing the content on your website, etc. These are all activities that are outlined within the Framework.

When you are planning, building and executing your website, ensure you build into your framework a follow-on plan that allows you to engage on all levels. You also need to constantly supply your website and all of your social channels with progressive, engaging and interactive content on all levels. Look at your sales funnel and find out where the attraction points are - then isolate these with your specific content and channel strategies. Consider how you look at SEO from a holistic perspective - you do need to understand the basics of what is important here, and how these will actually be able to help your business site.

Reflection/Action

Here are some questions to ask yourself, as you build your online empire:

1. Are you using "formal" SEO? If so, what are the specific goals that you have set out?

2. What other activities are you engaged in to bring traffic to your "goals"? PR, Blog, advertising?

3. How often do you write PR or your blog? Is this a weekly activity or whenever you get around to it?

4. How are people finding you now? From where are they finding you? Content based or activity based?

Defeating The Digital Delusions

Want to make real progress online? Change the way you are thinking about online. And, more importantly, check your assumptions at the door.

No, we don't all have these 'delusions', but we do have a way of thinking better and differently about the things that we take for granted.

Once you are aware of your own digital delusions, you can then be guided towards building a complete and comprehensive solution for the online aspect of your business.

List three of these digital delusions that you have encountered, that you know or think could be affecting how you work online. Are they dangerous? Do you suspect that they could grow quite bigger if you let them? Will they affect you further?

My Digital Delusion #1: _____

_____

_____

My Digital Delusion #2: _____

_____

_____

My Digital Delusion #3: _____

_____

_____

What other digital delusions have you encountered?

1. What is the delusion?

2. How can you identify it?

3. How can you defeat it?

Discover more details of the digital delusions and how you can overcome them.

Link here: breakthrough.digital/1

CHAPTER 3
THE 7 DISCIPLINES OF DIGITAL LEADERSHIP

"

By 2000, the machines will be producing so much that everyone in the US will, in effect, be independently wealthy. "

- Time Magazine, 1966

The 7 Disciplines of Digital Leadership

What do you really need to know to become successful online? How do you create influence online to create your breakthrough?

These are all big questions, with as many answers as you can possibly imagine. What I do know is that many wallets are emptied by people trying to provide this answer, without a solid foundation behind it.

That said, after spending over 14 years in the digital media space, it soon became clear what some businesses were doing online to be successful, while others were simply getting by, or worse yet - failing.

I've seen what can go right, and what goes horribly wrong. Yes, even from my own experiences, where I've made every mistake in the book.

Why does success online sometimes seem so far away? Why are some companies reaching significant levels of success, interaction, engagement and relevance that leave others spinning their wheels, and getting no traction whatsoever? Why are some businesses closing their doors?

Principally, it all comes down to digital leadership. What each one of us does, to guide and develop our complete online ecosystem, by taking control of it, not by simply following what others are doing.

What Is Digital Leadership

This is leadership of the digital kind.

Digital Leadership is fundamentally about developing remarkable online strategies combined with creative thinking in the online media worlds. It really is at the intersection of entrepreneurship and innovation. This is the point where businesses will show growth when they take up the cause to become a leader, not just a follower.

Digital Leadership is about delivering your remarkable value to your audience, across everything that you create and produce online.

Imagine what it would be like to be the leader in your industry, online. To have a remarkable business, that is engaging with your audience, has a fantastic customer community and significant online relevance. What if you could have a continuous source of sales leads and an ongoing commerce capability that was working extremely well? This really is whatever business aspires to, right?

The status quo isn't working however – businesses are struggling to get sales, leads, and engagement. Most websites are simple brochures on a messy old-time brochure rack or an old-fashioned bulletin board. It isn't a pretty picture at all. Many businesses can not believe nor understand why things are not working properly, or why they are not working as well as they were told by the so-called gurus and experts, without a lot of background to make these appropriate decisions. Winging it can work at times, but it helps to have some leadership and experience behind it.

In developing my own e-commerce businesses, as well as studying companies for this book, it really became apparent what some businesses were doing correctly, and what other businesses were still struggling with. It didn't always come down to being smarter, either. It really came down to some key things that they were able to convey a little bit differently.

Whether they knew it or not, they were able to define a consistent structure that they could then use in all things digital. This is where they were winning, as they were able to piece together all of the various elements of online, into a cohesive and congruent structure.

These are what I call the 7 Disciplines of Digital Leadership. They tie together the practical side of online, along with the strategic side, for long-term success.

The 7 Digital Disciplines came down to core areas of digital marketing, social media, strategy, SEO, websites and everything else in-between. No matter how you looked at them, they were always clear and consistent.

Those businesses that were able to see through all of this clutter and confusion were really, in essence, getting significant clarity in their everyday activities, and in their online business in general.

They had found, what I call, the digital leadership "sweet spot" – the place or position where multiple things come together simultaneously, and work in unison for the benefit of the business. Call it what you like, I tend to call it synchronicity. Their business just works well.

DIGITAL LEADERSHIP ARCHITECTURE

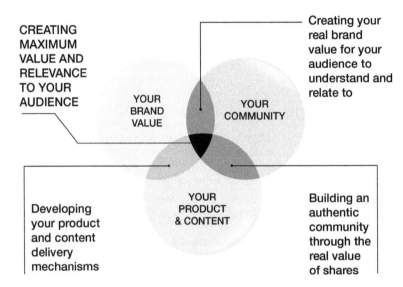

CREATING MAXIMUM VALUE AND RELEVANCE TO YOUR AUDIENCE

Creating your real brand value for your audience to understand and relate to

YOUR BRAND VALUE

YOUR COMMUNITY

Developing your product and content delivery mechanisms

YOUR PRODUCT & CONTENT

Building an authentic community through the real value of shares

Now, the industry has not been very helpful to businesses wanting to truly succeed online, as you always seemed to have to jump through another hoop, learn another buzzword, or hire another guru to get the job done.

And, as we've seen, often this process does not actually work.

What I also found was that the businesses that were working well online had a system. A process. A framework. An infrastructure that was the backbone of what they did.

Whether they realized it or not, it was a series of steps that they were implementing and utilizing, that were actually helping them with their online success. They were laying the foundation for some specific actions that were working quite well.

So how does this all fit together?

Well, as mentioned, I discovered that there were seven key indicators that some businesses were doing, and doing well online. So, I sat down with businesses and entrepreneurs and began to detail them out, and started to build a platform that qualified and quantified what was working well for entrepreneurs online.

7 DISCIPLINES OF DIGITAL LEADERSHIP

Successful businesses have discovered
these core elements to help them create breakthrough

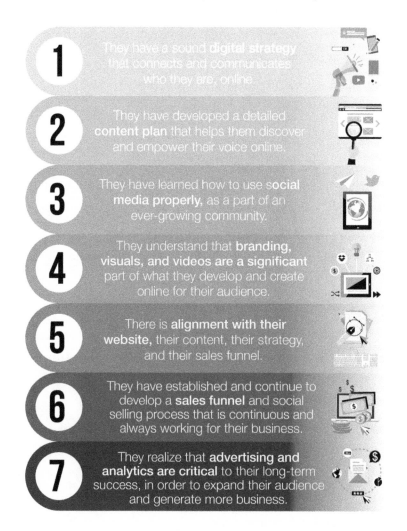

1 They have a sound **digital strategy** that connects and communicates who they are, online.

2 They have developed a detailed **content plan** that helps them discover and empower their voice online.

3 They have learned how to use **social media properly,** as a part of an ever-growing community.

4 They understand that **branding, visuals, and videos are a significant** part of what they develop and create online for their audience.

5 There is **alignment with their website,** their content, their strategy, and their sales funnel.

6 They have established and continue to develop a **sales funnel** and social selling process that is continuous and always working for their business.

7 They realize that **advertising and analytics are critical** to their long-term success, in order to expand their audience and generate more business.

These then became the Digital Disciplines, as they have come to be known as, that I have found work well for businesses exploring and exploding their online space.

These Disciplines will help you not only fully organize the online side of your business, but will also give you a new set of strategies and tools to better manage and maintain the whole online process, giving you the freedom to begin to work on your business, not in your business.

So, these are the 7 Disciplines of Digital Leadership that successful businesses have discovered that help them overcome the clutter and confusion of being online.

1. They have a sound **digital strategy** that connects and communicates who they are, online.

2. They have developed a detailed **content plan** that helps them discover and empower their voice online.

3. They have learned how to use **social media properly**, as a part of an ever-growing community.

4. They understand that **branding, visuals, and videos are a significant** part of what they develop and create online for their audience.

5. There is **alignment with their website**, their content, their strategy, and their sales funnel.

6. They have established and continue to develop a **sales funnel** and social selling process that is continuous and always working for their business.

7. They realize that **advertising and analytics is critical** to their long-term success, in order to expand their audience and generate more business.

What does it all mean? Well, start by putting each of these pieces together, and build upon them. It takes time, but it also takes an understanding of the factors that affect your online business, as well as the "process".

Everything of merit has a process that helps create the building blocks for growth and development. The 7 Disciplines of Digital Leadership are those building blocks that can, in fact, help you simplify what you need to be focussing on, online, without the headaches of everything else around you. It creates order from the chaos of the internet.

There has never been a better time to take control of your online business and make it as successful as you want. The 7 Disciplines of Digital Leadership create that architecture to build that baseline that moves your business forward.

This is what forms the structure of your business Breakthrough, which we will develop in this book. This is the framework that helps structure your strategy for success online.

Questions to Ask Yourself

1. What digital leadership disciplines are you strong at, and what can be improved?

2. How does each discipline affect you and your business?

3. What can you do differently to achieve success online?

PART 2

# #

BUILDING YOUR #BREAKTHROUGH

CHAPTER 4
YOUR DIGITAL DISCOVERY SELF
ASSESSMENT

"Remote shopping, while entirely feasible, will flop because women like to get out of the house, like to handle merchandise, like to be able to change their minds. "

- Time Magazine, 1966

Your Digital Discovery Self Assessment

Are you ready to use the 7 Disciplines of Digital Leadership to develop your breakthrough online?

Now we can start to apply these concepts to our own business, and start to implement the Breakthrough Digital Business Framework.

How do the Disciplines work? I'll start to lay this out for you, so you can see how competitive your business is, and what you can do to improve.

This self-assessment or audit can help further define where you currently stand, and what you can do to improve, which I will show you exactly how to do it in the next chapter.

It will show you how you score overall with your "digital leadership" and the empire builder part of your brain, with your business. It will help you understand as well that if it is not important, you don't really need to deal with it. The digital leadership assessment shows you exactly what is important, and what is not.

It is meant to give you an idea of where things are currently at with you and your business so that you can build your own individual, unique plan for your business, using the Breakthrough digital business framework. As I will show you, you don't need to be an expert in every single area, but this will help you outline what you are using effectively with your business online.

Is everything working together to build your business? Or, are you actually working against yourself?

Based on the disciplines of digital leadership, now you can find out.

Building an Online Breakthrough For Your Business

The methodology requires a new look at how you accomplish things online, and how you integrate these activities into your current business. Our methodology is not about starting from scratch, but rather putting the pieces that you already have, into a manageable and executable program that works for your business. The answers and details come from how your current business operates and implements. We simply provide the structure and framework to make your business function online, better.

This is an assessment of the key factors that are affecting you and your business online. Understand what you can do to create action, accountability, and process that helps you grow your business to where you want it to be.

This assessment is based on the 7 Disciplines of Digital Leadership that we learned about previously, as well as the award-winning Breakthrough process, and the core factors and understanding that have been predominant in helping successful businesses work better in the online environment.

The self-assessment is not meant as a complete "solution" per se, but rather to help you organize your digital platform, which works best for your business, in your market. We will develop the specifics of what to do next, in the following chapters.

Scoring Your Self-Assessment

There is a score for all of the seven main factors or "Primary Questions". This is based from 1-10, based on the relative assessment of how you compare to where the "ideal" position would be, with 1 being least competitive, and 10 being most competitive.

The scores are then added together to give yourself an overall assessment out of a possible 70 points. The supporting questions are simply reflective type questions designed to help you start to create a new roadmap in terms of what you can improve or make more efficient. There is no right or wrong answer, but rather just some key areas of your digital blueprint that can help you further develop your digital ecosystem.

Frame 1: Discovery & Strategy

Strategy is the key ingredient, as it creates the cohesion across all of the many confusing and seemingly disjointed activities of online. Your digital strategy serves as the foundation for your business to properly navigate online – from both your perspective and your customer/audience's perspectives. It is the intrinsic "why" of what your customer is purchasing and your audience is looking for.

It allows you to quickly convey the "essence" of your business to your audience, and understand the value that your customers are expecting from you. A strategy is not so much what you "do", but rather what value or qualities are in it for your audience. In other words, it is not always just about what your products/services physically are, but more so what value you provide with your products. In other words, how do you make your customer's life easier, better, and faster?

Primary Question

"I have a clear plan, blueprint or strategy that helps me understand where I am going, what I need to do, and how I define my business to my customers".

Score Yourself 1 to 10: _____

Supporting Questions

1. What are your online goals and objectives? Be specific.

2. How are you achieving these objectives?

3. What is your digital purpose?

4. What strategies do you use for engagement?

5. How do you deal with resource management - internally and externally? How much time do you spend developing your online digital ecosystem

Your Self-Assessment Outcomes

Take a few minutes to list the top 3 items that you can address with your business.

_____

_____

_____

_____

_____

_____

_____

Frame 2: Content Planning & Creation

Content is everything that you are "about" online, and that your audience can see, hear, feel, touch, interact, and engage. It is about the conversations that you can and should have with not only your direct purchasers, but also the people who are your bigger audience, and who can be a customer.

Content is not just about writing a good blog. It is also about creating and publishing your ideas of you, your business, your products, and your audience – what makes them like you, what value you provide. This can be conveyed in multiple formats, like social media, Facebook, YouTube, but also on your website, your advertising landing pages, webinars, downloads, gifts, etc. One of the biggest driving forces of the changing landscape of SEO is, in fact, content development and management. Sites that grow their content base, grow their rankings.

Ideally, you need to educate and inform your audience with your own expertise and knowledge. This creates awareness and relevance for you and your products. This is communicated by knowing exactly who you are talking to, in terms of customer segments or personas, along with the topics that you discuss.

Primary Question

"I know what I am going to talk about online, and when I am going to say it."

Score Yourself 1 to 10: _____

Supporting Questions

1.   Do you have a content plan? What is it?

2.   What are your five hot button issues?

3.   Describe your "voice" online

4.   How do you create content?

Your Self-Assessment Outcomes

Take a few minutes to list the top 3 items that you can address with your business.

_____

_____

_____

_____

_____

_____

_____

Frame 3: Social & Sharing

Social media needs to be recognized as merely a tool to develop your audience base. Social media is not a strategy. It allows you to communicate your message, through a strong strategy and a robust content plan. It needs to work together, with everything else that is produced by you and your business. It is not your business, nor should it ever be considered as your business.

You don't need to be everywhere, either. The social channels that you decide to use must be reflective of your overall strategy, as well as where your audience is located.

Social media is also about having a two-way conversation. This means that there needs to be hooks for them to both share your content, but also for you to engage in the conversations that are happening "outside" of what you are currently doing, and where your audience is predominately found. This means that it is beneficial to go to where your customer is, and start the conversation about your value. This is an evolving conversation that may not always start with your products, but more so with your value.

Primary Question

"I always have an engaged audience online."

Score Yourself 1 to 10: _____

Supporting Questions

1. Where is your customer on social media?

2. What are they doing?

3. What are your specific goals for social media?

Your Self-Assessment Outcomes

Take a few minutes to list the top 3 items that you can address with your business.

_____

_____

_____

_____

_____

_____

Frame 4: Branding: Video & Visuals

Branding is critical offline as well as online. It also serves as a conveyance of what you do, your values. And no, it is not just about your logo. Branding goes far deeper than that and presents you in all your glory. It is in fact your remarkable value that you are delievering.

Branding appears as part of the visuals and videos that you create and produce. And, they also serve as one of the strongest components of online digital strategy. Images and videos are shared and enjoyed far more than any other component of online.

As part of the further motivating messaging that is critical to your brand, images and videos should reflect everything that you should and want to talk about in pictures.

 Video and visuals are one of the key means for developing an audience online, by developing your own, online personality and brand to shine. Video content needs to include a regular weekly video episode of 3-5 minutes, highlighting the core business related content, as well as the personality of you and your brand. Image content, regardless of your business type, needs to have multiple occurrences weekly as well.

Primary Question

"I am always relevant with my audience and my brand across all branding, visuals and video content that I produce."

Score Yourself 1 to 10: _____

Supporting Questions

1. Describe your visual brand

2. What type of visuals are you currently using that represent your brand?

3. How do people visually find you, besides text-based search?

4. What does your visual brand represent?

Your Self-Assessment Outcomes

Take a few minutes to list the top 3 items that you can address with your business.

_____

_____

_____

_____

_____

_____

Frame 5: Website Alignment

Websites are meant as one of the spokes of your overall digital online framework – it is one of the critical components of your digital ecosystem. By themselves, they are just a simple method for transactions. However, when they are combined with your entire ecosystem online, they actually become a more integrated part. Your website serves as your main connection point to everything that is accomplished online. It builds your credibility, your relevance and awareness to your audience; it showcases your knowledge and expertise.

A website also needs to align with the overall messages of value that you are delivering. This means that it must be congruent with your strategy, with your content, with your social media, your landing pages and your advertising. Your audience is an extremely critical crowd, and won't feel at all amiss if they pass up your site, knowing that there are more out there just like you.

From the technical perspective, your website needs to have all of the elements necessary to grow your ranking and grow your relevance. It must be geared towards this, but at the same time, it must be descriptive and a "home" for your audience to come and visit, beyond the simple transactions. Proper ranking is based on a multitude of factors, but it is becoming more and more important to create a destination, an experience that everyone can enjoy, at any time.

As mobile devices have become ubiquitous, it is also imperative that you have a complete mobile experience for your audience when they choose to interact with you and your website. Even Google now adjusts or changes your ranking whether your mobile sites are delivering the best possible experience.

Primary Question

"My customers are always loyal to my business and my offers on my website."

Score Yourself 1 to 10: _____

Supporting Questions

1. What is the purpose of your website? Leads? Sales? Information? Be specific.

2. Does it currently work with your strategy and your content?

3. What is it that you feel does not work properly, or you would like to improve?

4. Do you have a content management system?

5. Are your website assets completely mobile optimised for all experiences?

Your Self-Assessment Outcomes

Take a few minutes to list the top 3 items that you can address with your business.

_____

_____

_____

_____

_____

_____

Additional Reporting Available

Want to generate some actual data on how your site is doing? Use these links to generate a quick website report

http://www.semrush.com/

http://www.woorank.com/

Frame 6: Online Lead Generation & Sales Funnel

The ultimate goal of having an online business is sales. Whether this is through acquiring leads or selling directly to your audience, the ultimate goal is to increase the value of the business. While this is a simple proposition, it is important to understand, as presented above, that only approximately 3% of your audience is "ready" to click and buy.

Having a proper sales funnel is about creating Return on Investment, or ROI. But again, it cannot be a simple transactional interaction, or the remaining potential audience goes unnoticed. You must have a sales nurturing cycle, where you bring people through your entire online ecosystem, creating that awareness and credibility throughout the process.

While e-commerce sites are designed to sell, they can also be considered to allow your audience time to get to know you, to tap into your knowledge and expertise. This is part of the 67% that can significantly grow your business.

The ideal sales funnel therefore needs to consider not only the single transactional purchase but also the ongoing awareness and relevance for your audience, along their buying cycle. And remember that it is about your buyer and their process, not so much you and your "selling" process. It is inherently different.

It is critical, however, to get your audience into your ecosystem. This includes such activities as "gifts", webinars, seminars, sessions, emails, planning activities, checklists, etc. It is necessary to manage and coordinate all of these activities to build a growing business.

Primary Question

"I have a consistent and continual source of quality leads and sales from my audience."

Score Yourself 1 to 10: _____

Supporting Questions

1. Define your sales, leads and buyers process.

2. How do you currently acquire new leads and new customers?

3. How do you respond and manage your leads?

Your Self-Assessment Outcomes

Take a few minutes to list the top 3 items that you can address with your business.

_____

_____

_____

_____

_____

_____

_____

Frame 7: Advertising, Analytics & Advanced Dashboards

Advertising is an integral part of an effective online strategy. Advertising needs to be properly coordinated with all of the other activities that you will undergo as part of your online framework. This means that all of the preceding steps ideally must be ready and complete, prior to moving onto the next "step". This ensures that the proper foundation is set-up, and will actually be able to work properly, with each other, not against each other.

In other words, if you set up an advertising program before you have a fully ready sales funnel (not just limited to an e-commerce funnel), and preceded further by a properly running EDM/email program, then money spent on advertising will be wasted. As you will not be able to engage the full process with your audience, and they may fall through some unnoticed "gaps" in the current or existing process in place. As mentioned, this is how most businesses have lost money – not just little bits either, but lots of wasted advertising budgets because they haven't connected their ecosystem together.

Ideally an advertising program would only take place once the key steps are completed in an overall strategic plan development. This allows businesses to send them to specific locations, whether that is a promo landing page, a landing page to gain subscribers, a product special, a video or visual, your specific social channel, or even a specific blog post that continues to engage and delight.

In terms of analytics, this is critical for your website in order to measure performance. Analytics is the methodology of measuring the activities on your websites. There also needs to be an active analytics package connected to the existing site, running at all times. This will allow for the proper analysis and subsequent action, to further enhance traffic and activity.

Primary Question

"My audience and prospects can easily find me online, and before my competitors."

Score Yourself 1 to 10: _____

Supporting Questions

1. How much do you spend on advertising on a monthly basis?

2. Have you used, or are you using online advertising? Do you consider it a success or failure at this point?

3. Do you know what is working on your website and what doesn't? How do you make any adjustments?

4. What type of tools do you use to monitor and manage what you do online, on a daily basis?

Your Self-Assessment Outcomes

Take a few minutes to list the top 3 items that you can address with your business

_____

_____

_____

_____

_____

_____

Your Total Digital Leadership Score

Add up all of the primary questions and write your score here: _____
Now, take a look at where you stand, and some general outcomes that
you can develop.

Your Score: 0 to 20

Investigate ways to further develop and define your digital footprint.
Are you spending enough time and resources to make it work? Do you
have a clear plan that you can implement? How are you really staying
competitive?

Your Score: 21 to 50

Understand that you can probably refine your digital approach to
be more competitive. Some significant changes may be needed,
with just a refinement of the seven key factors. Look at investigating
and investing more, in a greater depth of detail in all of your digital
programs, all your channels, and how you fit them all together.

Your Score 51-70

Fine-tune your approach, with such things as a refined sales funnel
and further integration with your social channels and your content.
Keep everything cohesive and coordinated to ensure that you can
deliver what your customer is looking for.

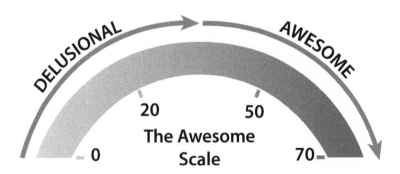

Some Additional Questions To Ask

1. From the list above, what elements of a complete, sound strategy are you missing? What ones do you have?

2. When will you implement the missing components?

3. What steps can you take towards putting these in place?

4. What has been your primary strategic focus for your business in the last six months? In the last year? What can you do differently in the next six months, and the next year?

5. If you had the opportunity to start from scratch, what would you include? What would you exclude?

Are You Ready To Take The Digital Leadership Challenge?

The scores that you create here are just "relative". They merely serve as a qualitative guideline to help focus your efforts as you build your online blueprint. We will give you the tools to enhance them in the next chapter.

Take a look at the online version of the self-assessment to see how you compare with others, and your competitors:

www.leadership.digital

Ready to learn how to implement? Head on over to the next chapter!

CHAPTER 5
YOUR BREAKTHROUGH DIGITAL
BUSINESS FRAMEWORK

*"" The nation's first home computer service,
which brought customers computer services
by telephone, is going out of business after 6
months because people don't trust
computers. ""*

- Williamson Daily News, 1973

Your Breakthrough Digital Business Framework

How would you feel if people were easily able to find and approach you online, to ask questions; and, that you were quickly able to nurture them into solid leads that then convert into sales or additional team members for your network?

As I've discovered earlier, breakthrough is a process, but also a mindset. It's a way of thinking. It's not just about putting a website up and expecting people to fill your PayPal account overnight. Most business leaders have this capability and desire to build a breakthrough, but sometimes are missing a few of the pieces to be able to put it all together. When you add in all of the confusion of what actually needs to be done, online, it can be quite a challenge to get to where you want to go.

The Breakthrough methodology is a Digital Brand Leadership Framework that creates the structure, the platform or foundation that allows you to build your masterpiece. It allows you to know and understand what pieces need to work together.

This is a digital workflow for businesses wanting to create transformation.

Think of it like building a foundation of what you want to do. There are a tremendous number of things you can do, but having a framework allows you to prioritize and focus on what is really important, and what is just fluff and unimportant. And online, it is critical to be able to focus on what is a priority, so that you can focus on your business, not in your business.

Without a framework, you simply have randomness and chaos - and can be drawn in any direction at any time. A framework helps you create that consistency and influence out of all of your activities online. It helps you build momentum.

Sadly, many businesses simply move slowly, with little forward vision and leadership, because they ignore the basics of a strong foundation; they neglect the framework to make it all work.

You wouldn't travel into a new city without a GPS (or map for that matter), would you? This framework is your instructor, your guidebook, and yes, your GPS for getting shit done online.

Although it takes some time to create a digital strategy platform, it will save you time and anxiety in the future. You need to play the long game for your business.

The goal of your business is to get people interested in what you do; which will then generate revenue and your bottom line ROI. It doesn't matter whether or not you are a direct selling business, a professional services business, an online retail e-commerce business, or even just a fan site – everything that you need to do online needs to make business sense, otherwise it is just a hobby.

More importantly, you want people to be able to find you, and to quickly recognize "you" for who you are. This is your own personal brand and your business brand – success, freedom; entrepreneurism at its finest. They are one and the same.

No matter where you go, or what your business is about, one thing is exceptionally clear these days. You and your business need to harness everything about digital.

However, contrary to popular belief, being online is not just about having a website.

Let me repeat that - having a website is not a guarantee for your success online. While 10+ years ago, it was, and you couldn't have a business without it, today it is more about all of the many other components of your online ecosystem that you need to manage and monitor effectively. You have to manage how all of the pieces fit together - this is why you need a framework.

It's about building a solid digital strategy that connects everything that you do online, into one congruent and cohesive plan for your ecosystem.

This is digital simplicity.

If you are currently a business that operates strictly in the "bricks and mortar", then you need to make a move online to truly create a distinct and unique level of operations with your customers and clients.

Like most businesses, if you are already online, then you need a specific, unique or individual way to fully engage and interact with your customers.

The Breakthrough Digital Business Framework essentially accounts for all of the seemingly disparate online activities you have and integrates them to achieve a cohesive message that fits precisely with what your business and audience needs.

The Framework is a content, events-based, active model that gets people in your "door" and into your network. It gets people to contact you, based on what you do online and will enable you to increase your online influence and relevance. It nurtures your ideal customer across their entire buying cycle.

All of the things that you need to do online, to build your online empire, can all be completed within this 7-step framework

From a digital strategy perspective, the seven disciplines of digital leadership cover everything that you and your business need to make that significant, remarkable breakthrough online. It does not matter what business you are in, or whether or not you have already been online.

It also doesn't matter whether Facebook survives for 509 years, or merely two more years. Or whether snapchat takes over the world...or doesn't. This is what a solid digital strategy does for you. It gives you the foundation for success.

This framework has a unique, structured and strategic approach that covers all of the components that work in the online world. It is not only a set list of clear and executable instructions, but a clear and underlying strategy that, when implemented correctly and diligently, will lead to business success.

Outcomes of the Framework

This is how you build your breakthrough online.

The Breakthrough Framework will highlight the process for properly building your business, engaging your audience and extending your influence online by defining:

1. How to define the best channels and social networks for your business.

2. How to develop your own specific content through videos and webinars, and utilizing other tools that actually work.

3. How to develop the knowledge base of your audience and lead base, so that you become the expert in your direct selling area.

4. How to learn to enhance your lead collection and generation system. So you've got customers or clients coming to your website? Learn what it takes to actually take them to the next step.

5. How to combine existing strategies with what you already know and do.

6. How to work with the major trends of SEO and social media, and every other type of online marketing that is out there.

7. How to create an effective online empire building strategy that grows with your business.

8. How to organize and utilize a detailed and aggressive strategy and management plan in order to become the leader in your field.

9. How to build and maximize your online influence, and convert that to users and partners for you and your business network, to build your business online.

10. How to focus on what will work for you and show you how to communicate and leverage that information extensively, in all facets of your business.

11. How to develop your online "influence", relevance, and, most importantly, get you customers or clients.

12. How to develop a comprehensive content plan that allows you to find your complete "voice", and deliver it in a timely and informative manner to your complete audience.

13. How to define your audience and target 'persona'.

14. How to define and more importantly deliver your remarkable value to your audience.

Elements Of The Breakthrough Digital Business Framework

Your business is not just about the "business". The primary goal of your business is to get people interested in what you do: to generate revenue and a bottom line ROI. You want people to be able to approach you online and offline, to ask questions; to nurture them into potential customers that convert into sales at some point in time. However, more importantly, you want people to be able to find you, and to quickly recognize "you" for who you are, not for someone else, or some other service. You need to build relevance and awareness. This is influence.

Your brand is about creating and developing an authentic community that is transparent and complementary to your client's daily lives and interactions; that are interactive and engaging with your products of your business capabilities. People want to invest and interact with your own personal authenticity.

It is about leadership in your industry; through action and thought-leadership of your skills and knowledge base, and of course your product lines. It is about connecting intrinsically with your clients to allow them to overcome their fears, and push them towards further manifestations of finding a safe and secure opportunity for them.

It is about creating the framework that allows your clients to clearly see and understand more through your knowledge, assistance and process.

Your clients enter your digital ecosystem, looking for a level of care and attention that is second to none. They won't be satisfied unless they know that they are dealing with the best. And, they are willing to pay the best, if they know that they can trust you to take care of their needs. It is about trusting you with the ability to enjoy their own business. You need to own the entire process, the entire framework, the entire platform.

This is the framework that we will be using for building your online empire. Combined, these steps cover material that is critical to how you organize, manage and operate your business online. It is about organizing, building and enhancing your online influence, with all the tools and resources that you have at your disposal.

Essentially, the steps are:

Frame 1	**Strategy Development** Learn how to craft a key strategy to guide all your online activities.
Frame 2	**Content Planning** Learn how to develop your "voice" online, for your audience.
Frame 3	**Social & Sharing** Understanding what you need for a proper social media engagement.
Frame 4	**Video & Visuals (Branding)** Create proper branding, visuals and key video that tells your story online.
Frame 5	**Website Alignment** Understand how to connect all of the elements of your website with everything that you do.
Frame 6	**Sales Funnel** Create a working sales process so that you can actually generate sales/leads, and positive ROI.
Frame 7	**Advertising Analytics** Increase you audience awareness with key advertising, and improve your online activities by analyzing your results.

Frame By Frame – The Breakthrough Digital Business Framework

Of course, a framework needs to be implemented – it needs a methodology – so let's take a closer look. The good news is that you don't necessarily have to start everything from scratch. You may be surprised at how much online activity you already undertake, and may need to just organize or reorganize. From the digital self-assessment earlier, you obviously have done a few things to get the ball rolling.

In some cases, it may simply be a case of "marshalling your troops" and harnessing the power of what you already have at your disposal. It will help you manage your ecosystem and fundamentally reduce the complexity of what you are doing.

Frame	Focal Point	Theme	Core Criteria and General Activities To Complete
1	Discovery & Strategy	Online Empire Building "Disco" Discovery and Strategic Alignment	• Audit and Understanding of Current Capabilities • Establishing a strategic architecture • Social media strategy review and questionnaire • Social Media workshop review • Customer identification and discovery
2	Content Strategy & Deployment	Content Planning, Creation and Development.	• Building Your Story online • Designing your content • Scheduling, Timing & Delivery • Concurrent Needs of SEO • Press Releases and Media development
3	Social & Sharing	Social Networking and Sharing.	• Channel Prioritization and Selection • Channel set-up and establishing your foundation • Channel strategies to get maximum value for your business • Cross-channel propagation • Coordinating and scheduling your content.
4	Video & Visual Content (Branding)	Video & Visuals.	• The importance and ease of video • How to create video content • Creation & Production • Placement of video channels and cross promotion • Setting up your SEO Requirements • Usage and placement of images • Technical requirements of images • Management of images and sharing

5	Website Alignment	Website Alignment & Congruency. Create and evolve your web presence	• Understand and implement website goals • Restructure site as needed for "gifts" and "product for prospects" • Create congruency • Embodiment of proper sales funnel • Back-end SEO • Content Development • Mobile Responsive
6	Sales Funnel	Online Lead Strategies. How to create the sales funnel that works.	• Lead Development – Ascending Transaction Model • Webinars as lead generators • Product development in the online environment • Social Networking advanced lead generating strategies • EDM activities and list building • Content distribution in your lead generation • Effective Online Sales funnels • Affiliate Marketing
7	Advertising, Analytics & Dashboards	Advanced Online Empire business building strategies and tactics.	• Online media buying and advertising on Google Adwords, Linkedin & Facebook • Content channels to expand your reach and your control • Online Response strategies • Analytics & Measurement • Measurement, Tools & Dashboards to use to control your online influence and response

Want to build a complete and comprehensive digital platform?

Let's get into the detail of how to build your influence with a solid digital strategy.

What Is It?

"Frame 1" consists of discovering what your business is about. It is your 'why' that resonates with your audience. It is important to delve into the brand essence of who you are as a business, and what you do. How do you understand and discover your brand essence? You need to ask and answer the question "what are you about"? Then, translating what you think and do into a strategic architecture that will help you align all of your digital and online activities.

Do you understand the micro trends that are growing and shaping your business? What about your customer? Are they "following" the same trends that you are? While it may seem like a simple problem, as a business leader you need to ensure that the trends around you and your business are complementary to what your customer and audience are looking for, otherwise your business will eventually fade out.

The strategy is the overriding plan that allows you to align what you do online with your actual business. Strategy is not the same as actual "tactics"; a strategy is the overall plan that you are undertaking, not the specific activities that you will carry out.

You need to be able to have congruency between what you think you are about, what you want to be about, and what your customer thinks you are about. Only once you have this alignment, will you be able to build your breakthrough success.

Doyle Buehler

What You Need To Do

Through a series of strategic planning exercises, you will come to quickly understand that what you are about is sometimes different from what you perceive yourself to be, or what your customer perceives you to be. The understanding needs to be more about what the underlying philosophies of your business. Sometimes, digging deep into what you're not about will lead you to a better understanding of your company.

You will need to review and answer the following questions:

1. What are 'we' (your business) about?

2. What do 'we' do best?

3. What makes it work?

4. What is the value that we will provide to our customers? Today, tomorrow, next year?

5. What are we good at? What are the skills/competencies of your business?

6. What are we good at? What do we need to be better at?

7. What is your "experience" about? What will your visitors take away from your website?

8. What does your customer "look" like? What are the customer baselines and trends, such as Who is your customer? What are they doing? Where are they doing it? What are they looking for? How will you engage them in their space?

Take the answers to your fundamental questions and create three key pillars or concepts and understandings about your business. This then becomes your "Strategic Architecture". Use your strategy and understandings across all your implementation to create congruency and a sense of "self" and your brand value.

Follow-through Actions

Take some time to understand what the overall value of what your audience is looking for. Do they simply want your product or do they want convenience, status, simplicity, access? What do they achieve by purchasing your products

or services, compared to your competitors? How do they feel when researching and purchasing? What is the essence of your business? What value will you deliver now, as well as down the road?

Investigate your long-term business goals - both customer side and business side. This can be used to help the business focus on some long-term changes in customer responsiveness to your products and services. How will you attract customers in the long term? What partnerships are you developing to help expand your audience base? How do you inform and delight your audience over the long-term, and further, how can you demonstrate your essence, your value, your knowledge of the industry as a whole? How can you connect with the 67% of your audience that can account for growing sales?

Ask your customer what they are "really" looking for. Understand what motivates them and then convey this into additional knowledge and expertise that can be utilized by your target audience. Conduct a simple survey of the different stages of research and purchase behaviors that may lend some insight into your customer motivators.

Take The Next Step

Download the full strategy questions from www.breakthrough.digital/1

The Digital Framework #2

Content Planning

Learn how to develop your "voice" online, for your audience

What Is It?

Content, in essence, is what you post and put on the web. Everything that you have ever produced gets indexed and relates to what you and your company has put online. It's not just about your blog, either. It's about everything that is about you and your business online. If you haven't posted anything online, there really is nothing online to tell your story.

While content also contains photos, images and videos, which will be covered in Frame 3 and Frame 5, the core content at this stage is the actual text and words that you put in place, linked to what your business is about. This applies not only to your website but in everything that you produce online, including the text on your website.

Content is the core of Search Engine Optimisation (SEO). SEO does not need to be excruciatingly difficult or complex. SEO is really just about connecting what you say with what you produce online. The important thing to remember is that without content, the search engines will not find you, and hence, your customers will not be able to find you either. You will be irrelevant. Correction, you are irrelevant without your content.

Online writing is surprisingly underutilised by the majority of businesses and entrepreneurs. It should, in essence, be considered as fundamental as existing activities, like sales, operations and marketing.

It is imperative that writing about your business be prioritized to the same level as these activities, as it carries the same – and sometimes more – weight in your business.

Having a personal or company blog is critical for the success of your business as it creates the linking point for all of your content that you subsequently create online and share with others. If you do not have a company blog, then you need to create one. If you do not know how to write one, then you need to learn.

"Blogging" is unfortunately viewed by most as 'something else' and that does not help with the building of the business. This attitude needs to change in order to maintain relevance. You need to write as if your business depends on it, because, even though you may not be aware of it yet, it actually does.

The main thing preventing you from writing and producing content is probably not that you can't write, but rather you are not sure of what you should write or talk about. Correct? This is called the "white-board" syndrome - getting ideas out of your head is sometimes the hardest part. However, once you start, things begin to move forward quickly. The way to make producing content easier and much more effective and timely is by looking more at what you do and putting some structure to it.

The good news? You don't need to write down and "type" a blog – that is really old-fashioned. Instead, think of ways of getting your ideas out of your head – complete some audio recording, some video recordings, that can then be transcribed and used in all forms of communication. So, when I talk about blog content, I'm really referring to your own content and the many different formats that you can take it down, to get it into the hearts and minds of your audience.

Content no-longer needs to be one-dimensional. You can create it and amplify it in everything that you do. You just need to generate it.

Doyle Buehler

How much content are you actually generating for your business?

Your blog is connected to everything, and if not, then you need to make this adjustment. Your core content also consists of your website, social media, video, visuals, gifts and downloads; these will be covered later. Your blog is a distribution channel that needs to be at the core of what you do, from where everything else flows, including:

1. Video discussions

2. Press releases & media

3. Images and sharing

4. Social and sharing connection

5. Syndication (other bloggers/posts)

6. Email content marketing

7. Industry news and publications

8. Document hosting

9. Podcasts

10. Content transcripts

The search engines are constantly scouring the Internet for content about you and everything related to your business, and, more importantly, your competition. This is your "relevance". This is all about how your customers are actually able to find you online. If you don't produce and post your own content, then someone else will, and your business will not be able to develop online, as there will be no relevance.

Content is important, but it also needs to be relevant to you and your business, as well as attributed to you and your business, which is how you stop being 'invisible'. Google is more and more looking for a great user experience, and putting the text and content into context. If you are not able to do this, your competitors already are.

A general industry 'understanding', is that about 90% of online content is just consumed amongst everyone, and created by a select few. Nine percent is actually copied and re-published by others, for such things as social media links, etc. This leaves a surprising 1% of content that is actually created as the source by writers, entrepreneurs, etc. Once you realize this, it is easy to understand why creating your own content can develop your business and relevance online, as not many people are doing it – most people are simply copying.

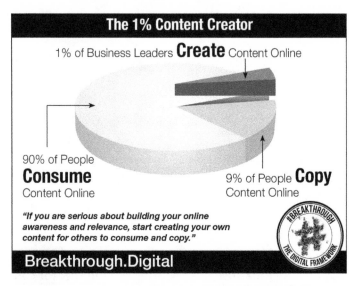

Content will raise the awareness of you and your organization; it's as simple as that. You will be able to kick-start a conversation internally or to wider public audiences, as well as capitalize on a topic trend to introduce your company as a ranking expert. You can also supply news about your industry or company that is no longer provided by mainstream media. And, you can get information to vitally interested niche groups about your product or service. Content helps others find you and your business, whatever that may be.

What You Need To Do

Understanding content is the easy part. Building
content is the part that will take some work and
dedication. The other core aspect of content is
actual "curation"; how you build, maintain, reuse
and repurpose your content.

The big thing is that you don't need to produce only your content,
all of the time. You also don't need to always publish just your own
content. Get in the habit of sharing content that your influencers
share. Then begin to create and publish your own material. Add it into
your content mix. You will always need a balance, but don't fret about
getting everything all at once. Creating and producing content takes
time. So take the time and produce good content, but get it out there.
It does nothing by sitting on your computer.

And no, I am not condoning simply copying and pasting your
influencers content as your own. Share the content of your influencers
as well as the content that your audience likes. This is how you start to
build a community and connect with your audience.

In developing a content plan, you will need to become proficient in
the following:

- Content Strategic Alignment. How does the content fit with your
  own specific goals and strategic plans?

- Developing Themes for your business.

- Content Development

- Content Scheduling

- Attribution & Setting Up Authorship

- Setting up a Blog

- Press Releases

- Content Curation and Usage (frequency)

- How to write shareable content

- How to place content across the Web

- How to write content that is more about building a community and does more than just sell

- Develop and understand your customer. Create personas or personalities that are your ideal customer. Create relevance by talking specifically to them.

What about keywords? Yes, keywords are important, but keyword "stuffing" is not going to work. What is the "key" about keywords? Talk about what you are best at, and your own keywords will appear. What is the content of your normal, day-to-day conversations? These are the same conversations that you will have online, complete with all of your own keywords.

If you don't think that you know what keywords you need to use, then here are some tools for researching further:

- SocialMention.com
- www.stumbleupon.com/tag
- Technorati.com/tag
- Ads.youtube.com/keyword_tool
- www.hashtags.org

Keep in mind that the content on your entire digital domain needs to be conversational. People will be reading about what you have, and making an assessment of you based on this.

Here are some types of content that you can create:

- Articles
- Blogs

- Case Studies
- ebooks
- Images
- Info-graphics
- Microsites
- Mobile content
- News releases
- Podcasts
- Research
- Slideshows
- Social
- Traditional media
- Video
- Webinars
- White papers/special reports

Questions to consider:

Take a look at these content questions and activities, and complete them as best as possible.

1. Using your refined strategy, list six core topics of information that you will discuss online.

2. Further, separate your six core activities into three sub-topics or topic specialties.

3. Create a content calendar. For each subtopic, complete content activities and writing each week. Post each of these as blog posts within your company or personal blog. Include all other types of content in your overall content plan.

4. Identify the various personas that are part of your audience and customer base. Who are they? What do they do? How can you describe them?

5. Share your blog posts across all the channels that you will develop.

6. After 18 weeks, create new topics, subtopics and a new calendar.

7. Develop a list of 12 topical keywords that you will use; these will form part of your core content. They are what you will need to use throughout all manifestations of your content.

Follow-through Actions

Develop an understanding of the different customer segments, and what content interests them is key to defining how to create a sales conversation with them. Try to group your customers into separate "personas" that you can then market and communicate directly too.
It gives you a target to discuss with, instead of seemingly random conversations. See how far you can "describe" them, then talk with them.

Map out what you would like to say, what your audience is saying/ wanting, and when you would like to say it. This is the basis for a content plan. By structuring it by topics and by dates, it allows some structure, which can then be implemented quite easily over time. Having a schedule will also save you time and money, as you can quickly refer to it and say "I need to write about x,y,z, today". Further break down the schedule by each channel, so that you can then navigate and manage all of the channels easier. Look at ways of enhancing your content, through downloads, free gifts, checklists, what you need to know, mistakes people make in selecting bar fridges, etc.

Look at communicating on all of the different channels that you are currently utilizing or set-up. However, focus on the channels where your customer is at so that you don't dilute your resources unnecessarily. Keep the overall message consistent across everything, based on your new, refined strategy, and your content plan. Consistent, quality content generally improves your overall SEO rankings. Can you communicate and educate as well, through other channels, like webinars on "creating the perfect backyard"? This basically works by connecting all of your thoughts into content that you can deliver, across multiple channels.

Take The Next Step

Download the full Content Questions, content canvasses, and Content Brainstorm sheet from www.breakthrough.digital/1

The Digital Framework #3
Social & Sharing
Understanding what you need for a proper social media engagement

What Is It?

Social media networking is about connecting you and your business with your customers and potential customers through your social media channels. Connecting with your audience, however they are defined, is critical to your overall business success. Without an audience, there is no business, no matter how good you might be, or how perfect your product or service actually is. Enabling a specific strategy of business building online requires that the sharing side of the online interactions are developed and leveraged.

Social media is, however, just a tool. It is one tool of many that you need to build an effective online business. It is a medium that you can use to interact and engage with your audience. It is, in essence, no different than the use of television to broadcast content, ideas, and of course advertising. It is not your online business either; it is part of the whole.

The significant difference today is that social networking is more about a two-way form of interaction with an audience and brands online. No longer is marketing "pushed" onto the viewer. Now, people are only interested in what they find and "pull" towards themselves, based on their interests and activities. This is all part of the relevance aspect.

What about social selling? This is the integration of social media with "sales", and building an understanding of how these channels can work together. Social selling is a topic unto its own, but at the end of the day, you still need to build a community of your audience through social media, as well as have a platform for selling. Both of these are covered within the Breakthrough framework detailed in this book.

Brands that can leverage this overriding philosophy of social media and social selling being a tool, and have allowed content and ideas to be "pulled" by their audience, are the ones that can build very large communities online in the social networking space. They are able to interact and engage with their audience in a manner that promotes the concepts of sharing information and knowledge across their full product range and activities. 'Good' brands using social media don't "sell" their audience "buys", based on how they feel about the brand.

There are a significant number of channels in social media that allow for this participative, opt-in marketing. As part of the strategy of your business, it is important to understand where your audience will primarily be. Where do they work? Where do they play? While Facebook is one of the tools that you might consider, it is important to understand that there are other tools that may work better for your business. The further evolution of social networking means that the available channels are becoming more and more specialized as time progresses. Find out where your audience is, and the then you can build out your specific channels.

What You Need To Do.

In order to create an engaging and inviting environment, it is necessary to create content that is related to what your audience enjoys and understands. Your message has to resonate with your audience or it will simply not be able to sustain itself. Remember Frame #2 - this is why we talk about content before social media & sharing. We have to understand what to say and to whom before we can contemplate the 'where'.

While social media channels seem to change quite regularly, there are some primary categories of channels that can be used, including blogs, micro-blogging, social networks, image sharing, and video sharing.

These are some of the basic steps for developing and building your social media channels:

1. Understanding the basics and types of social networking, and how each one may work in your business.

2. Channel analysis – knowing what to use, when, etc. Where is your customer?

3. What specific 'social' needs do you require for your business? How does this fit with your overall, revised strategy?

4. Setting up your channels so that they are connected.

5. Content Development - placing your content everywhere.

6. Community Development. Look at sharing not only your content, but also the content of others. Share in the conversation with others in your "neighbourhood".

Then...

1. Decide on what social network channels will work best for you, your business and your audience.

2. Connect your social media channels with your website and your online goals.

3. Allow for sharing in a bi-directional manner. Cross-promote content. Connect all your social media channels with each other, and with your primary website and sales funnel.

4. Post to your core knowledge platform. Become the expert in your area.

5. Distribute your content across your social channels.

6. Complete all of the "about me" and SEO sections in all of your social channels so that you can create the necessary links and relevance for you and your business.

7. Implement your content plan. Post to your schedules and post content on all of your social channels.

8. Interact and connect with other, complementary businesses; comment and compliment on what they are saying.

Follow-through Actions

Ensure that, at a minimum, people have an immediate way of connecting with you, across your social channels, in every direction. Start with having links to your social channels on your main pages. Build out a content comments system that then shares back to their social channels. Ensure that your content that you create can be shared, with simple share-based connections points for your videos, images, blogs, etc.

Create consistent branding throughout all of your
channels. Use the same images, color, style that
you know works for your brand. Ensure that all of
the profiles set up are complete – that they have
a lot of textual descriptions (for SEO), as well as
links to your main site.

Use social media from both directions. Find out where your audience
is, and start contributing to the conversation in their space. Don't
make it a hard sales conversation, but a statement of values that you
provide. Lead them, with your content, to understand how they fit.
Consider the 67%. Consider the growing field of social selling. Create
conversations in your social media channels, with content that reflects
your audience's interests and needs.

Take The Next Step

Download the full Social Media Planner Questions and structure sheet
from www.breakthrough.digital/1

The Digital Framework #4
Video and Visuals
Create proper branding, visuals and key
video that tells your story online

Branding is not just about having a logo. It's about creating a value
identity – and video and visuals are critical for achieving this.

Part 1: Video

What Is It?

Video is one of those technologies that is far underutilized for
business purposes across the web. Did you know that YouTube gets
3 Billion views per day? If you are not creating video, including live
videos, then you really are not doing business the way that it needs to
be done.

Video allows you to showcase who you are, and what you are about. It
creates a greater understanding of a person, their business, and their
personality. It is a way of connecting that simply cannot be matched
in any other medium. It is a relatively easy way for people to get in
"touch" with you and your expertise.

Every business and entrepreneur has content that can be translated
into a video format. This allows for sharing content across all channels
that you then have, with just a link. Video allows you to step above
your competition, to become a showcase of you and your skills and
your business.

How Does It Work?

Video is visual. It is where you create the content to instruct and share your knowledge, to increase your relevance and to lead people to action. Whether it is about training or a simple display of knowledge and expertise, video gets you "out there" in a powerful way.

Remember, however, that "video for video's sake" is not that effective. It is necessary to plan ahead and produce relevant content that represents who you are and what you do. You can then leverage your videos in weekly episodes, which people will come to rely on you from you. Create and use video as part of your overall content planning.

What You Need To Do.

Here are some key concepts that are important for creating effective videos and video content:

You are Your "Brand" - Know yourself; present yourself as you are, along with all of your quirks and idiosyncrasies; your individual character. Don't worry about what people will think. Just film it! Present yourself as your brand and what you have to offer.

It doesn't need to be perfect. Just get it out there. It doesn't need to be a Hollywood production. Just get it out there.

Timings - YouTube analytics consistently show that people are more likely to click play on a shorter video, and more likely to 'stick' with a video if the end is in sight. For example, if you publish a six-minute video, people will stop watching at the four-minute mark, but they'll likely stay to the end of a five-minute video. Always be as concise as possible and within a specific timeframe that gets your points across. Aim for roughly 2-3 minutes per video.

Great Audio, Video & Lighting - Be sure not to neglect clear audio over video, or adequate lighting. All aspects need to be the best that you can afford. Quality is paramount. While non-professional videos are sometimes cute and quaint, better quality does mean that they will become more valuable over time. Don't be afraid to start though, even if you don't have high-end equipment and lighting. Having said this, do ensure that you have good quality audio. Poor audio is the best way to have someone desert your video very quickly.

Accountability - Set goals and timelines and stick to them. If not, involve someone you can trust to help keep you on track. Create a video at least once every week or every two weeks. Schedule the same time and same place, so that your audience starts to get in tune with your consistency.

Knowledge - Keep your knowledge base working so that it is productive and beneficial to your audience. Avoid too much jargon and technical information.

Then...

1. Plan your video outreach – develop your content plan as detailed in Frame 2, but specifically for video.

2. Creating a weekly schedule that fits into an "episode" of your special content.

3. Establish your channels on YouTube, Vimeo, or other hosting services.

4. Film your episodes on a weekly basis; record short videos of about 2-3 minutes. Set one day a week to upload your weekly episode, and ensure this is done.

5. Create a live feed that defines your remarkable calue and content.

6. Broadcast your video and share it across all of your other channels. Use your blog as a primary means of sharing your videos, and then link into all of your other channels. Promote the video in all of your status updates, and all of your posts.

7. Always complete the full descriptions, tags and keywords for your videos, whether you are hosting them yourself, or on YouTube or Vimeo. Even consider getting the video transcribed, which is now offered on YouTube to add to your content development and availability to amplify. The search engines can't actually 'see' video, hence you need to be as descriptive as possible, to enhance your relevance.

Part 2: Visuals

What Is It?

Images are the "currency" of the online world. Even if you think that your business is not necessarily "picture friendly", it is critical that you move towards increasing the level of image representation, both from a website basis and also from the social networking side of things.

The biggest misconception? You need to be a photographer to benefit from using photography of your business. Yes, even accountants can use it. Think of the visual medium in everything that you do - your webinars, your computers, your people, your properties. Everything can be a picture for your visual brand.

While it does change from time-to-time, recent statistics from Facebook indicate that the items that have the highest share equity are, in fact, images, then links, and finally, text status updates.

Moving into a visual world online for your business can be done quite promptly, as there are many services and apps that will help and assist with developing your message.

Here are some critical aspects that need to be developed for the use of photographs in your online business:

- The importance of images for sharing - Photos can quickly move from user to user.

- SEO & Images - Search engines are not yet able to actually "see" photos, so you need to enhance them with text-based referencing for search engines. Give them a filename that has your keywords and company information; fill out all of the ALT text, title and description tags for your images, within your site.

- Tools & Apps for Images - What app works for your business and your user base/audience?

- Taking Good Photos - If you need help with photography, take a quick photo course. Utilize free photo editing software.

- Use of Word Art - Convert your infamous quotes of the day, into word art as an actual picture.

- Creative Uses - Look at how photos can be used in all aspects of your business. How do you convey your marketing message photographically?

- Branding - All images that you own and create need to have your own branding and URL. This allows for future views to be able to re-connect with you and your brand.

- Infographics - These create the opportunity for unique, branded, knowledge-based graphics. Look at how you can implement these types of images to further enhance your business.

How Does It Work?

There are many different photo sharing social networks, apps and programs that allow you to increase your level of brand awareness.

Additionally, as photos are shared online, it is important to ensure that your photos generate positive SEO, through a variety of methods. These include:

1. Save the filename as your brand name or website name, along with 2 or 3 adjectives that describe what the photo is actually about.

2. Always put a watermark on your photographs with your web address.

3. Utilize tags, alt text, meta descriptions and other text-based descriptions and referencing to further allow search engines to locate your images. Include your URL in all of your positioning.

What You Need To Do

Answer the following questions about your business:

1. What photo-sharing, social media site works for your business?

2. How can you use photographs of your business? What products do you have? How does your service business photograph activities?

3. How will you name the photos and use tags to further generate SEO relevance?

4. How will you put an emphasis on photos in your regular social network channels?

Then...

1. Create an image database that is online and connects with your URL. It also needs to detail out all of the photos and images that you use for sharing.

2. Add visuals to your content plan and implement them across all of your channels.

3. Create incentives for sharing your visual content. What ideas are you conveying in your visuals? How do they work and how do they interact?

Follow-through Actions

Utilize a large depth of images and videos. These should all be assembled with your new overall strategy and content plan, to help you focus on the details of everything. Use images and videos to not only show the product but show how the product or service is used, what it can mean for your customer, etc. Images for strictly product purchases can also be used as the "lifestyle" surrounding your business and what you are trying to create.

However, it is quite useful and practical to create separate images that convey the value, and the lifestyle that is important to your audience. Consider creating lifestyle videos as well, that again convey your products in their lifestyle – think beyond the typical product shots, and more of the value statement of how their life is more complete with your product range. Engage the emotion of their lifestyle in all of the visuals and videos. Create inspirational visual & video messaging that connects with what your audience wants to achieve – not just product based. Consider using "infographics" and other designed visuals that tell a story, with your product being the focal point.

Optimize all the images and videos for SEO/search. Ensure that all videos and images have a full, detailed file name. The images should also be able to be accessed separately, for sharing; with each image having the share capability.

Utilize branding on all your images, so that your audience will soon be able to recognize your visual brand. This can be as simple as putting your logo and web address on every single image that you create. This allows for anyone to begin the process of recognition, regardless of where they actually saw your photos.

Take The Next Step

Download the full Brand development guide and visual and video content planner from www.breakthrough.digital/1

The Digital Framework #5
Website alignment
Understand how to connect all of the elements
of your website with everything that you do

What Is It?

Your website is the lifeblood of your online business. While you may
have all of your social media channels in place, all your video uploads
performing, all your photos loading on Instagram, everything relates
back to what your website does, and how well it performs. Your
website is where you will actually make money for your business.

Your website is the engine of your business. However, you still need all
of the other components to make it work, together, and to get to your
destination.

Without it, you are non-existent. Having said this, a website won't
work well on its own - it will need the "supporting infrastructure" of
other online tools to make it work.

While you can have a Facebook page, it is difficult to run a business
completely on Facebook. Your own web page gives you the ability to
create your own environment, under your own terms; it conveys the
essence of you and your business.

Your website is the mainstay of your online digital identity. It is your
foundation and your home base. It's where the majority of purchases
are made and where people search you out. Think of it as being no
different than your own retail store, business, or coffee shop.

How Does It Work?

Your website needs to align with all of your various channels. It is your primary channel and platform that everything is built upon. It needs to be first class, and it needs to be put together with order and a clear understanding of your overall online business strategy.

It fundamentally needs to align with your strategy, and everything that you produce. Your website must have congruency with what you have now built with your revised strategy and strategic architecture that we worked on earlier.

If you already have an existing site, you need to ensure that you create the alignment needed across every other channel and every page. This means that your web pages need to be congruent and that the information is consistent across all channels and platforms. The message that you deliver needs to be clear, but importantly, it needs to be aligned with everything that is about you and your business. You also need to start to think about your sales funnel, and how you will put these pieces in place as well.

Keep your website "clean" from a design perspective. Your website needs to reflect the overall branding that you have and are developing over time. Ensure that you have exit and entry points and that you are developing strong primary and secondary calls-to-action to enter your sales funnel. Forget about using your "Contact Us" page as your primary business interaction. As we have learned, we need more, much much more, to nurture your audience along their complete buyers journey.

What You Need To Do

Your online presence must be congruent across everything that you build online. This includes, more particularly, what is happening on your website along with mobile.

Doyle Buehler

Take a look, and ensure that this is what you have:

1. All social channels need to be displayed. They need to be connected, but also to ensure that people can share your content with their own community.

2. Ensure that you have sharing capabilities across all of the different components of your website. Share to Twitter, Pinterest, Facebook, or whatever channels you are using.

3. Include your blog in your own pages. Use this as your PR message, as well as for your content distribution.

4. Your visuals should match between all different channels.

5. Ensure that your analytics package is setup, and you have specific goals embedded into the process.

6. Create your sales funnel, with specific downloads, webinars, and of course, purchase points throughout all of the different stages of your site.

7. Create easy to use navigation.

8. Use lots of visuals, as well as key videos for your pages.

9. Understand your overall strategy and how it affects your website.

10. Regularly change your "static" content on your pages, usually at least every 1-2 months (this is beside the weekly updates of your blog).

11. Complete the back-end SEO, such as using complete Meta descriptions.

12. Always utilize your core keywords throughout your website.

13. Feature video that highlights your sales, purpose, goals, core business, etc.

14. Ensure your site is mobile responsive.

15. Use an SSL for security and audience confidentiel.

And, most importantly, your website must be congruent with your strategy. It must provide you and your audience with everything that they need to complete the buyer's journey.

Additionally, there will be other aspects and activities that you will need to take into consideration, when aligning, implementing and utilizing your website.

Linking - Establishing and creating links to your website, complementary sites and all of your social networking channels. This is "connecting" all of your various channels and activities across everything online.

Local Marketing - As mapping and GPS becomes an integral part of people's day to day lives, your business can leverage this capability effectively in all of your online activities, including developing and enhancing your SEO.

Mobile Marketing - There are currently more mobile devices than people on the planet. Most people are mobile-enabled, to allow them to be constantly connected at all times. How do you connect with your audience in the mobile environment, as part of your brand experience?

Building a website is not an easy task. It needs to be viewed and designed from multiple angles and multiple uses. Here are some of the basic elements that you need to accomplish in the actual design stage of your website, to build in that congruency:

1. Headline – What is the main focus of your website?

2. Sub-headline – What are the other details or messages that you need to convey?

3. Benefits & Value – Why would people do business with you? What kind of value can you deliver? Not features, but real, solid value.

4. Primary Calls-to-Action – This is where your goals come into play. What specific actions do you want your visitors to undertake? Utilize 2-3 calls to action that reflect the various buying stages of your audience.

5. Features – What are the features of your products that you want your audience to quickly recognize?

6. Customer Proof – If you have any customer testimonials, use them to build your credibility.

7. Success Indicators – What makes your solution the best out there?

8. Navigation – Ensure that any person can get to any point on your site within two clicks.

9. Supporting Images - All your visuals need to support your overall messaging.

10. Gift Offer – Provide some initial information at no cost or obligation to your intended audience, to help begin entry into your sales funnel.

11. Resources – This is your own library. How do they download your checklists, source lists, guides, etc.?

12. Secondary Calls-To-Action – Connect and engage with your social media channels. Ensure clients can contact you quickly and easily, and that they can sign up to your email list, or download some key knowledge pieces.

13. Conduct an SEO scorecard. Look at: keyword targeting, title tags, meta descriptions, internal anchor test, inbound links, outbound links, image alt text, social links, social sharing widgets. Look at using the newer form of SEO, including schema.org

14. Create a "Responsive" site that allows can automatically configure itself for mobile devices and tablets.

15. Create landing pages that allow you to create niche content - which we will detail further in Frame 6.

Regardless of what platform you chose to build your site upon, a properly designed and developed website will usually take four weeks to create. This is usually as a result of getting all of the content and designs created, as well as the back-end configuration for e-commerce. Take the time to build a design first, and then convert it into a website. If you are using WordPress, or other DIY site builders, like Wix, move away from the standard templates and create something that closer fits you and your vision, as well as your customer's journey with you.

Your website needs to be part of a constantly evolving process. It will never be "finished", in that it should be a constantly developed by adding new content, and adjusting the different aspects of your site. Why? Well, the search engines also look at how often your site gets updated, as this is usually a good indicator of currency and recency. Refine it more and more as you go along, knowing that you do not need to start with the perfect website.

What you need to understand before moving forward:

Ask yourself the following questions about the overall design, development and implementation of your website:

1. Will you be completing the work internally or externally?

2. Will you be using a professional web designer?

3. What key features do you want and need for your website?

4. How will you generate leads and sales from your site?

5. What type of content will you distribute? What free gifts or promotions will you offer to visitors?

6. How will you track all your visitors?

7. What are your site goals?

Then...

1. Align your website with your new strategy, content plan and website goals.

2. Write a website specification that allows you to fully explain the types of features and capabilities you want your site to have.

3. Start building, adding to or re-designing your website. Continue to develop and grow it over time. Keep it live, interesting, visual and dynamic.

Follow-through Actions

Coordinate your "revised" strategy and content plan into your website. Include a more consistent level of content production. Include all of the social media features. Create more of a destination with your content and the overall structure. Integrate a sales funnel process that can include your audience in their lifestyle of your products and services, such as checklists, guides, etc. for download.

Utilize affiliate partners as well as Google Merchant capabilities for your product feeds, to grow your sales, as well as your overall audience. Continue to grow backlinks, based on partners and affiliates.

Utilize newer SEO capabilities, such as Structured Data Markup Language, which is a search engine tool used by Google. Remove any "over optimized" sections of the current meta tags, as Google may penalize your site for this.

Take The Next Step

Download the full website specification development planner from www.breakthrough.digital/1

What Is It?

Despite the Internet being a premium sales kit for every business and entrepreneur, there are a lot of businesses who are not actually harnessing what it is that they do online in terms of a cohesive sales process. Understanding that your business needs to treat each and every fan, customer/client or person, as actually part of the sales process, or sales funnel, is critical for online success.

Despite that, as mentioned, this is one of the most misunderstood aspects of business online. 98% of businesses are set up the exact same way that they were when the Internet first came into being over 20 years ago. This was without understanding the true evolution of the customer that has happened since then. Yes, I'm talking about the "Contact Us" page, once again. Don't let this artefact of 'generations' of web development get the better of your business. Yes, you still need it, but you need more; you must help them to the next step of the buyer's process of your ideal persona.

A website without a built-in sales process is what makes the difference between a successful business and a mediocre business.

A sales funnel is the process by which you bring your web users closer towards an action or a sale. A sales funnel can be directing the user towards a specific action, such as downloading an ebook, opening a specific sales page, making an email request for a test drive, encouraging them to visit your store, or anything in between.

In more recent times, many businesses have also moved towards "social selling"; social selling advocates meanwhile indicate that this is the best way, and only way to sell, by using the platform of social media. Social selling is not just about selling through or with social media – it needs to be much deeper than that. Social selling is actually quite simple, yet we still miss the main elements of it from a digital business perspective. Yes, you need to align your social media towards selling, create a process to be able to capture leads and move them towards the sale. Yet, we are still missing out on some of the fundamentals of sales and funnels and nurture sequences. It's not quite as easy as getting a pro account with Linkedin; social selling needs the same objectives as presented here – create an actual salesfunnel and nurture sequence that progresses your prospects towards your ultimate goal. Regardless of how social selling is defined, you'll still need all of the elements as part of the breakthrough framework to really help make this happen.

If you operate an online e-commerce store, your obvious goal is a transaction. However, it is important to understand that your customer is not always ready to make a purchase through your online channel. In that case, it is important to feed them into your larger funnel each and every time they enter your site and nurture them towards becoming a customer - preferably a repeat customer.

If you are more of a service-based business, your sales funnel should be to book an appointment with you, download an ebook that you have written or are offering, or anything similar that allows a contact or push to an end action and continue the conversation. You will also need to "productize" your service with specific packages in order to make the purchase transaction easier to accomplish.

Every time a visitor touches your website, whether or not they make a purchase, they need to be guided along the way towards your ultimate goal of a sale or some type of contact.

How Does It Work?

Visitors are "captured" and guided towards your business goals. Every link, status and activity should be part of the sales funnels you are creating and generating for your business.

Components of a sales funnel can include:

- Download an ebook
- Link to a specific page
- Email or call directly
- Make a purchase
- Make a booking
- Send out a tweet from your page
- Specific social actions
- Webinar registration
- Inquiries
- Leads
- Sales
- Referrals

Also think about these as goals or outcomes, to get to where you want your customer to head. Some of these outcomes can include:

1. Elevate Brand perception
2. Establish thought leadership
3. Drive customer engagement
4. Provide better customer service
5. Increase customer retention
6. Build a larger referral network

What You Need To Do

1. Establish a method of contact for your audience such as email list management and auto responders.

2. Outline and detail what your sales funnel is. What is your outcome? What are your goals?

3. Decide how you can use online advertising to grow interest and awareness in your online activities?

4. Identify what you consider to be a "goal". Is it a specific action that you want your customer to do? Once you have identified and created your goals, you can then establish the benchmark by attaching a specific Google Analytics goal.

5. Decide on what webinar services you can use? What topics do you need to address? How do you tie in your webinars with your overall content planning from Frame 2?

Then...

1. Establish your product "gifts" or "lead magnets", available for download.

2. Create your "Product for Prospects", such as webinars, workshops, seminars.

3. Ensure you have your core service created as a product, and as part of a package.

4. Establish your communication channels through email and auto responders.

Follow-through Actions

Implement email marketing follow-up cycles
for all sections of the sales cycles. Base it on
your revised strategy and content, however,
ensuring that you deliver exceptional value to
your audience, and that it is congruent with your
overall messaging. In other words, don't just
send out emails because you have their email addresses – only if you
deliver real value to add to their day.

Even with all of the automation tools out there, keep in mind that you
can only automate the process; you cannot automate the relationship.

You must continue to grow the 'real' relationship in order to bring in
new business.

Create additional points of entry into your sales funnel for pre-and
post purchasers. This can be accomplished with downloads, gifts,
checklists, etc. that directly connect you to your audience. Utilize
specific landing pages for specific lifestyle goals and offers.

Utilize your social and sharing platforms to entice sales and interest in
your products, and move them into your overall sales process. Include
links and discussions related to your audience's goals to your site
and promotions, in social media. This needs to be aligned with your
overall content and social media plan.

Take The Next Step

Download the full Content Questions and Content Brainstorm sheet
from www.breakthrough.digital/1

The Digital Framework #7
Advertising & Analytics
Increase your audience awareness with key advertising, and improve your online activities by analyzing your results

What Is It?

Advanced online strategies include the utilization of tools and methodologies that allow you to further refine your business activity and ensure that your business is continually evolving online. Think of it as a checkpoint, that you can now see how you are doing, as well as put in place that extra level of promotion to expand your circle of influence.

As we've also discovered and alluded to, advertising before this point in time along the Online Empire Project can be considered somewhat futile. Why? Well, it comes down to having the pathways and the infrastructure to support advertising campaigns. You can't just send clicks to your homepage; you must deliver an experience within your own ecosystem that is congruent with what you are in fact advertising. This is where millions are lost - creating campaigns and advertising that your online business can't actually support. Now whoever, you can send them anywhere - specific videos or visuals, specific content on your site, specific landing pages or training, new infographics.

Now you can control and manage the conversation with advertising.

Frame 7 consists of the following core activities that will further develop and enhance your business and how you continue to grow and build it:

- Setting "Goals" and measurements with Google Analytics - While these have been established with your website and sales funnel, they also need to evolve further during this stage. These are the measurable goals or activities that need to move people through your sales funnel, but also to be able to measure and identify what is happening.

- Advertising on Facebook, LinkedIn, Google and any other advertising networks.

- Analytics & Measurement - Analytics is the combination of data analysis and statistics. In order to be truly effective and understand what is going on, you need to be able to get the information that helps you make business appropriate decisions online.

- Managing Multiple Channels - While it is important to have a focus in all of your online activities, it is also necessary to use a variety of channels to further develop your online influence.

- Toolkit/Dashboard - As your business expands, and you become more engaged online, you will need to ensure that your messaging is unified, and more importantly, cohesive with your overall message. Efficiency is key, as a dashboard allows you to message consistently across multiple channels, simultaneously.

- Coordinating offline and online activities - One of the downfalls of modern business is the fact that there appears to be a firewall between offline and online activities. Your offline messaging must be congruent with your online messaging.

- Reporting - While this ties in with analytics, it is important that you structure information that is valuable to you and your business. What are your KPIs? What are your business objectives? What are you actually able to measure?

- Return on Investment (ROI) - Now that you have all components working together, you can actually develop and enhance your ROI. Utilizing an ROI measurement is now something that will work, and make sense. The reason that a lot of businesses stay away from ROI is simply that they are scared of what the result may indicate. Once you have all of the pieces in place, then you will readily be able to calculate a proper ROI in all of your online endeavors.

How Does It Work?

These final strategies allow you and your business to further refine your business activities and become more precise in their execution. Creating congruency between all activities is critical to ensure a sound strategy and create unity with your customers.

These activities also ensure that you are enabling your customers across all of the channels that you operate in to act, giving you a competitive advantage.

What You Need To Do

Answer the following questions for your additional understanding:

- How do you measure your online success, in terms of traffic?

- How can you make your online workflow efficient?

- How are you actually measuring and analyzing what your customer is doing online with your website and your other online properties? How do these relate to your KPI's?

- What Dashboard and CRM can you use that best fits with your overall goals and the outcomes you want for your website?

Then...

1. Set up analytics for your website. Analysis what is important to you and your business.

2. Create advertising campaigns that are focused on a very small niche market, in order to create the biggest interest and gains. Test your campaigns. Establish niche landing page through such services to unbounce.com, to further enhance and learn from your marketing and advertising efforts

3. Organize your social media and blog posts with a dashboard and management tool, such as Hootsuite, or Cyfe.

Follow-through Actions

Enable all of the analytics features of your site, including audience profiles. In terms of measuring how well your site and activities are doing, look at and investigate utilizing initial Measures of Performance factors, such as Traffic into sales funnel; leads generated (such as through downloads); Followers and engaged users; Sales and registrations.

Test your assumptions with online advertising. If it doesn't work, it doesn't mean that it never can. It just means that you need to refine your assumptions and refine your messaging to your audience.

Utilize a dashboard or console, for the management of campaigns and activities. This can be used through such tools as Cyfe, where you can customize all the activities that are pertinent and important to the day to day operation of your business. A "console" can also be established with Google Analytics, although it does not always have all of the features for complete management.

Ensure campaigns are congruent and move people towards your e-commerce and sales funnel goals. This can entail the creation of specific product landing pages, so that it corresponds directly with what the audience has clicked on. Slight improvements of campaigns could be developed by adjusting bid prices slightly (downward), while still maintaining close, existing ranking. Remove all of the poor performing campaigns, which are not revenue focused. Look at advertising (once your digital platform is developed), onto other channels, such as Facebook and YouTube with Promoted posts/ads directed to your activities and specific gifts, sections, webinar registrations, etc. Review your Adwords activities on a weekly basis, to ensure that campaigns are meeting specific goals and objectives.

Take The Next Step

Download the full advertising planner questions and worksheets from www.breakthrough.digital/1

Some Additional Questions To Ask

Building a digital breakthrough is, in essence, knowing what to do and when. An established platform will give you the confidence to move forward without hesitation, knowing that you, in fact, have the knowledge to succeed. Here are some additional questions that you can ask, to further enhance your Online Empire project.

1. Where can you lead your community to, next? What do they really want from you?

2. How can you better convey your overall brand value to your audience?

3. What are your competitors doing better than yourself? How can you overcome this?

4. What is really holding you back from being a true digital brand leader? Is it resources? Time? Management? Whatever it is, don't let it slow you down.

PART 3

# #

ACCELERATING YOUR #BREAKTHROUGH

CHAPTER 6
BUILDING YOUR ONLINE
ACTION PLAN

"These Google guys, they want to be billionaires and rock stars and go to conferences and all that. Let us see if they still want to run the business in two to three years."

- Bill Gates, 2003

Building Your Online Action Plan

The power is in your hands. I've shown you exactly how you can create your breakthrough online, by developing a strong and robust digital ecosystem. Now, let's close with a few other supporting roles that you can put in place to ensure that you are playing the long game in digital.

Setting Online Goals

The framework that has been created in this book allows you, the business leader, to be able to organize your methods of online management. By putting things in a clear order and outlined manner, you will be able to understand what is important and stay away from the things that are not. We're almost there.

The whole framework is only as strong as the sum of its parts. It is important that each of the components is looked at individually, yet worked on together, as a group. While some sites, for example, may not have an e-commerce capability, it is still as important, if not more so, to be able to create specific goals or outcomes of what your site needs.

Nothing can work properly unless you set up specific goals for your online environment. The components reviewed previously will help you shape what it is that you need to do. At the end of the day, however, you need to ensure that you have a very specific set of "goals" or targets that you put together, specific to your business. This will be very important to further building the structure around your business.

The importance of goals/actions is critical for ensuring that you have a means to improve and build upon what you are already building with your online business. Specific goals will help you begin to build a measurable level of interaction and engagement. Without goals, you really do not have a means for measuring whether you are actually successful or not. And, without a measure of success, you can question why you are in business.

Your goals can be such things as:

1. Download a free "gift", such as a free report, checklist, white paper, or anything that develops the contact with you and your audience.

2. Watch a specific video.

3. Make a purchase

4. Answer a survey

5. Go to a specific blog page

If you don't have any online goals or actions, then you really don't have a business, and your website is basically just a brochure site, adding little actual value to your business. With no goals, there is nothing to achieve, and nothing to actually measure if you have made it or not. You need to set up some goals within your online domain to further enhance the online experience, as well as create measurable, quantifiable actions for your audience.

Keep in mind that goals, do not always imply items specific to your website. Rather, your full online goals for your entire digital ecosystem can also include a lot broader goals, such as:

1. Producing valuable content that informs and entertains your audience

2.   Creating webinars that educate your audience

3.   Developing online training programs

4.   Creating tiered membership sites

5.   Create specific landing pages

6.   Develop and implement new gifts on a regular basis

Questions to consider for your business:

1.   What current goals do I have on my website, if any? What are they?

2.   How can I segregate specific goals or actions with my online plan and development?

3.   What goals do I need to put in place? What is important to me and my business?

4.   What are some targets for each of these goals?

5.   How will I implement my online goals?

6.   How will I measure my online success?

7.   How do I integrate my goals with Analytics & measurement?

8.   How am I contributing positively to the ongoing creation of useful and valuable content for my audience?

Create A Master Schedule

Create a giant master content schedule or table that lists all milestones and approximate details of each, along with the timings (weekly, daily, monthly, etc.). For simplicity, start with a 3-month schedule that will allow you to begin the steps to create consistency across all channels.

Your schedule needs to include:

- Autoresponders

- EDM

- Video posts

- Photo posts

- Blog posts

- Gifts, downloads

- Webinars, workshops

- Social posting

- Videos

- Visuals

- Gifts

- Advertising

- Personas

- Themes

- Website

- Events

- Landing pages

When you are building your schedule, consider what channels you will be using, as well as how you will be delivering your message. Produce content that is regular, focused and appeals to your specific personas of your core audience by keeping in mind the following issues:

1. Channel(s) of distribution

2. Type of content

3. Relation and context of content

4. Timing of content (day, month, week)

5. Persona that you are speaking to

6. Themes and topics that you can develop

7. Frequency of posts/content

Other Resources

There are some online resources that are available to develop further and enhance the Online Empire Framework.

Download all of the new tools from www.tools.digital

Here are some basic tools to get you started.

Link	#Breakthrough Framework	Item
www.toggl.com	Frame 1: Strategy	Time Tracking
http://basecamp.com/	Frame 1: Strategy	Project management
http://www.tickspot.com	Frame 1: Strategy	Time Tracking
http://www.blogdash.com	Frame 2: Content	Sourcing of blogs
http://www.pagemodo.com/	Frame 3: Social & Sharing	Facebook Image Creator
http://audiojungle.net/	Frame 4: Video	Royalty based sound files for videos
https://marketplace.visual.ly/	Frame 4: Video & Visuals	Create infographics for visuals, for your sales funnel
https://magic.piktochart.com/	Frame 4: Video & Visuals	Create infographics
http://visual.ly	Frame 4: Video & Visuals	Create infographics
http://www.ereleases.com	Frame 6: Sales Funnel	Press Release services
http://www.clickwebinar.com/features	Frame 6: Webinar Software	Clickwebinar service
http://www.instantpresenter.com	Frame 6: Webinar Software services	Instant Presenter
https://www.timetrade.com/td/dashboard.jsp	Frame 6: Sales Funnel	Online Time Booking
http://www.jotform.com/form-templates/	Frame 6: Sales Funnel	Creating forms for online use, surveys, event registration, etc.
http://unbounce.com/	Frame 6: Sales funnel	Create landing pages
http://www.instapage.com	Frame 6: Sales funnel	Create landing pages
http://www.agorapulse.com	Frame 7: Advertising & Analytics	Facebook management suite
http://www.involver.com/	Frame 7: CRM - social media management	
http://www.gatective.com/	Frame 7: Analytics	Analytics verification

#Breakthrough - Resources

You can also download the following kits and planning templates from www.breakthrough.digital/1 - all for free!

1. Strategy Planning Questionnaire

2. Sample Strategic Architecture

3. Content Planning Questionnaire

4. Website Specification

5. Blog Template

6. Social & Sharing Outlines

7. Other worksheets that help structure your business effectively

Your New Digital Leadership Scorecard

Now that everything is in order, we need to take a look at where things are for you; what your new baseline is, and will continue to be.

So, consider the following seven criteria, and see how you are positioned:

1. What is your core strategy and "essence" of your business?

2. How are you going to structure and deliver your content across all of your channels?

3. What social media channels are best for your business, and how will you connect with your audience?

4. What branding visuals and videos will you use to further enhance your brand strength?

5. Is your website now aligned with all of your goals, your strategies, your content distribution, and your branding?

6. Have you put in place an effective funnel and nurture sequence to lead your audience through the buying process?

7. Are you using measurement to ensure that what you are doing, is correct? Are you now advertising more effectively because of your improvements in your platform and target audience?

Once you have completed the Breakthrough methodology, and gotten some wins under your belt, go back to:

www.leadership.digital

And, retake the Digital Assessment every 6-9 months and find out how you now stand with a better understanding of digital, and how to put it all together for you.

My how you have changed!

What have you been able to improve? What have you been able to change? How can you now create your breakthrough for your business?

CHAPTER 7
RULES OF ENGAGEMENT

" *There's just not that many videos that I want to watch.* "

- YouTube cofounder Steve Chen, when the site featured only a few dozen videos, 2005

Rules of ENGAGEment

Now it's time to get shit done. You have in your hands the exact tools and methodology that will make a difference in accelerating your business - all of the elements, all of the pieces, all of the strategies that work - you have got everything that you need. So make it happen - no excuses.

Now that you have connected all the pieces, here are several things that you need to do:

1. Calculate and utilize ROI. You have an understanding of what your costs are. For those of you who are obsessed with ROI - go calculate it. If you don't care about ROI - don't calculate it. Either way, you will see exactly what you need to do now.

2. Continue into the building stages of your business. The foundation is set, now you need to continue to build your "home". This means that you have to continue to develop your channels and maintain and build your schedule, among other things. Create a master schedule that you can use to break down your content, and to break down all of the activities that you need to complete.

3. Create a schedule for all of your activities, every three months. Three months is an excellent time period to be able to properly gauge what you are doing and see what may or may not be working. It is an opportunity to change things if you feel that they are not working properly.

4. Follow us and join our growing online community. We will have regular updates to our program, new insights into our methodologies, additional checklists and other things to keep the delusions at bay.

5. Set up your online goals - and look at how you are actually meeting them as a minimum, and exceeding them to your best ability.

Remember that you can't just set up the entire program and let it out to graze. You need to be smarter than the rest and manage it regularly. Continue to refine your tactics for your overall strategy; continue to put all of the tools that are at your disposal, in their right place; continue to streamline what you have done and what you need to do.

If you want a breakthrough, you need to break through.

Break through the crap

Break through the clutter

Break through to what your audience really wants

Breakthrough in what you deliver with your value, consistently

Breakthrough with your business

Unleash Your Remarkable Brand Value Online.

CHAPTER 8
PLANNING YOUR STRATEGY & MARKETING

" The truth is no online database will replace your daily newspaper, no CD-ROM can take the place of a competent teacher, and no computer network will change the way government works. "

- Clifford Stoll, author, 1995

Planning Your Strategy & Marketing

As we are approaching the end, I'll keep it simple. Strategies are needed. A strategy helps you align everything that you are doing, and how you are doing it. This then allows you to focus in on your marketing initiatives.

Shiny object syndrome is real, and most businesses are victims of it. It's not about joining the next Facebook, nor the next Snapchat, nor Social selling. It is more about how you integrate all of these aspects, one by one, to deliver consistency across everything that you do.

Strategic marketing is not easy, but it lays out the platforms that you really need, to get the job done, well.

Imagine what could happen to your business, if you were able to properly and effectively understand everything that could happen, and everything that you could do to make it happen? Strategy gives you that option.

If you can lay out the framework of the Breakthrough Digital Business methodology, in advance of what you are planning and doing, then you will have a real plan, a real initiative that will give you the focus that all businesses can use more of. You will be less inclined to follow the leader or follow the shiny new thing.

There is of course a distinction between planning and doing. They are obviously both extremely important, but typically the "doing" gets the priority, as that is what is making the money and keeping the business alive and running.

Imagine what could happen if you look at more of the planning so that you can actually be doing more, and doing more, better than you are? This is one of the fundamental concepts of business - while working in your business is important, working on your business is even more important.

The framework that I've presented, allows you to do just that - think more strategic, be more strategic, which will help you grow a better business for the long-term.

Here are a few steps to take, to ensure that you embody strategy throughout your business, helping you grow it to an even bigger and better place.

1. Look at the long-term effects of what you are doing, and planning for. Digital is the long-game.

2. Review your strategy at least once per year. Tune in to what your audience is looking for.

3. Don't be afraid to adjust your strategy, based on a better understanding of your market

4. Use your strategy to guide your business decisions, not the other way around.

5. Regularly test your assumptions.

CHAPTER 9
WHAT TO DO NEXT

" *Neither RedBox nor Netflix are even on the radar screen in terms of competition.* "

- Jim Keyes,
Blockbuster CEO, 2008

JOIN THE CONVERSATION

Join The Conversation!

Find me, here:

 www.about.me/doylebuehler

 www.facebook.com/doyle.buehler

www.facebook.com/thedigitaldelusion

 au.linkedin.com/in/doylebuehler/

Linkedin http://www.linkedin.com/in/doylebuehler

 http://instagram.com/doylebuehler

 www.twitter.com/doylebuehler

 http://www.slideshare.net/onekanzuru

 Google+ http://plus.google.com/101726301477581347234

 Youtube http://www.youtube.com/user/doylebuehler

 Pinterest: http://pinterest.com/doylebuehler/

Discover more resources and links:

www.breakthrough.digital/1

Want to send an "old-fashioned" email? Please email me:

doyle@dept.digital

Breaking Digital iTunes Podcast

Please join me for my regularly scheduled podcast on iTunes, where I interview digital leaders, giving you fundamental strategies of how to adjust your digital ecosystem.

www.breaking.digital

Slideshare

Take a look at some of presentations that discuss the many topics of digital marketing and online strategy talked about in this book and beyond:

http://www.slideshare.net/onekanzuru

Facebook Fan Page

https://www.facebook.com/thedigitaldelusion

THE WORLD'S BIGGEST ONLINE TOOLKIT

Digital Monkey Wrench - Finding The Right Tools For The Job. The World's Biggest Online Toolkit.

The Hottest SEO, Social Media & Digital Analytics Tools For Marketers

I've been spending a lot of time, trying to find tools that will help entrepreneurs. Sadly, tools are all over the place, with little organization for anyone to use or understand. Big long lists of tools, that had no reference nor relevance.

I'm changing that. I've created a list of tools that you can use, that actually tell you when and where you should be using the tools, according to the 7 Disciplines of Digital Leadership, where you can build your online empire. So yes, when you are going through the different steps, and want to enhance what you are doing, take a look at the tools that we have compiled, to help you directly with each section that you are at.

Giving you some peace of mind, and extra time that you don't have to use hunting forever for that one simple tool.

Keep in mind that tools are just tools. Find the best tool for the job or even the one that works best for you.

Rules of Tools

1. Find the tool that is specific to each segment that you are at. There is nothing more confusing than finding a tool and not sure how to integrate it or where it can fit.

2. There will always be a better tool out there. Find the ones that work best for you.

3. Keep an eye on your budget, most tools start free, but can all add up quickly

4. If you like a tool, tell other people

5. Tools are just tools - pick the right one for your job.

6. You don't always need the shiniest tool in the toolbox

7. Tools need tactics - understand why you are using the tools, and what benefit you are getting from the tool

And, the final Maxim on tools:

While you can automate the transaction, you can't automate the relationship

In other words, tools will only take you so far. Use them to help, but they never can replace the effort behind the tool. Hammers don't work on their own.

Tools Sorted By Strategy And Workflow

Yes, I've organized the tools by when you need them, in relation to the Breakthrough 7-step process. This allows you to focus squarely on getting shit done, in an easy and structured manner.

How Do I Find These Tools?

Take a look at our digital marketing tools site:

www.tools.digital

Please add some more if you know of some, or share with others that know that they need to get a new toolbox.

Doyle Buehler

EDUCATING FOR DIGITAL & ONLINE BUSINESS

Education is important in everything that we do. We need to teach everyone the principles that have been laid out, so that everyone can learn from them, and take the industry back from the brink.

Education and training has been a central focus throughout my life, and I value the ability to teach others. I have spent many years teaching and mentoring entrepreneurs, students, and people who are just interested in the exciting world of business. I've taught young students who didn't really know what business was about, to people who have decided to take on a new career challenge.

How does education fit in with the #Breakthrough?

There is a tremendous amount of misinformation and misguidance out there. How do we stop this or simply reduce it?

1. Learn about your own business.

2. Understand how the pieces fit together. Educate yourself about what is important - only you can be the expert.

3. Invest the time, energy and resources needed to establish yourself and your activities.

4. Question who gives you advice and why they are doing it.

5. Educate others. Let them know what the digital delusions are, and more importantly, how to overcome them by systematic, simple solutions. Consider establishing delusion debates with your business peers to isolate other problems that are present. Consider teaching others just getting into business, what they need to be aware of. Help them avoid making the same mistakes as you have in the past.

The only way to eliminate the delusions is to understand them. The only way to understand them is to learn about them. The only way to learn about them is to educate others. Tell others how they can overcome these digital delusions.

Want to contribute to the education side of the #Breakthrough to ensure that we can all start to learn what we really need to know?

Go to www.breakthrough.digital to connect with some of these additional resources:

- Download the complete ebook for free
- Find out if we are speaking in your area
- Put on a seminar or workshop in your city or area
- Join Our Team
- Join an introductory webinar
- Find a workshop in your area

Need to purchase bulk editions of #Breakthrough and other educational materials at an educational discounted price? Please contact us at education@dept.digital

Discover all of the tools and planning activities that will further enhance your digital platform.

FURTHER READING

Further Reading

Degrees of Separation in Social Networks: Reza Bakhshandeh, Mehdi Samadi, Zohreh Azimifar, Jonathan Schaeffer
Retrieved from http://www.aaai.org/ocs/index.php/OCS/SOCS11/paper/view/4031

Google, Zero Moment of Truth Research Paper
Retrieved from: http://www.google.com.au/think/collections/zero- moment-truth.html

Handley, A., Chapman, C.C. Content Rules. John Wiley & Sons, NY 2013

Nahai, Nathalie. Webs of Influence: The Psychology of Online Persuasion. Pearson, Sydney 2012

Niels Bosma, Sander Wennekers and José Ernesto Amorós. The Global Entrepreneurship Monitor (GEM) 2011 Global Report.

Priestley, D. (2011). Become a Key Person of Influence. Hertfordshire, UK: Ecademy Press.

Roberts, Kevin (2005). Lovemarks: The Future Beyond Brands (Expanded edition ed.). New York, NY: PowerHouse Books.

State of Mobile 2013 Infographic, Supermonitoring.com, retrieved from: http://www.supermonitoring.com/blog/2013/09/23/state-of-mobile- 2013-infographic/

Velosa, Maria. Web Copy That Sells. American Management Association. NY 2013

OTHER PRODUCTS & SERVICES

What is Dept.Digital?

#Breakthrough is more than just a book and a way of creating business. It is an "anti" Agency. It is a way of doing business. It is a new wayof thinking and implementing for businesses wanting to become Leaders in their industry.

Dept.digital is creating a new awareness and understanding of what is needed to succeed online. It is about mastering the digital domain and creating clarity and confidence online for your business.

It is about helping entrepreneurs and business leaders cut through the clutter and confusion of being online, so that they can become remarkable.

There has never been a better time to take control of your business, and become the online business leader that you are.

We leave entrepreneurs feeling awesome, online.

Please go to www.dept.digital to continue to stay informed and stay involved, and find out what works for your business:

- Email sign-up list
- Videos
- Scheduled Webinars
- Scheduled Workshops
- Digital Delusion Gifts

Want to grow your business further? Ask us about Licensing, Franchising and coaching services.

We have come a long way. We started out understanding the industry as one big delusion. Now we are more in tune with what we are supposed to be doing.

It's still not going to be easy; but it is going to be much clearer for you. Comprehension and knowledge is key.

The journey doesn't stop here either; you need to keep going. Develop your online empire. Make your project work like it should. Become the entrepreneur that you know you are.

We've seen it before. Remember when someone exposes to the world how magicians and/or illusionists trick people, all of the other magicians or illusionists get mad at him for spilling the beans? We've given you the "reveal" moment. Now you have that "a-ha" feeling, and subsequently you will get a much clearer understanding of what you have just accomplished.

Well, we are about to spill the beans and ruin it for all of those ad agencies, SEO, PPC and online "support" companies trying to trick you into buying their services. The ones that are keeping you fooled into paying them; the ones that keep you delusional in running your business online...

You now know what to look for and what to look out for, as you become a truly remarkable entrepreneur.

"It's not magic. It's business."

Take what you have learned, and use it. Manage it and make it better. Change what you are doing and improve what you can do.

YOUR FREE DIGITAL STRATEGY ONLINE TRAINING COURSE

Your Free Entrepreneur Online Training Course

Want to take your understanding to the next level, to further build your digital platform? As a reader of this book, you are entitled to receive my free training program, which includes dozens of key downloads, over 20 hours of videos and complete instructions to build your complete digital platform and grow a successful business online.

Go to breakthrough.digital

FREE PDF VERSION OF THE BOOK

Download the Free PDF Version of The Book

Get a digital PDF copy for your smartphone, tablet or ebook reader. Go to breakthrough.digital/pdf to get your free copy now.

ABOUT THE AUTHOR

About The Author

Doyle Buehler has coached and inspired many in the areas of digital leadership, online marketing, social media and digital strategy. His primary goal is to help businesses become Outrageously Outstanding Online. He is an author, entrepreneur, speaker and online business brand strategist, and is at the intersections of entrepreneurship and digital innovation. A former military pilot and Aerospace engineer, he has spent 14 years in the business world where he has grown multiple online & e-commerce businesses and start-ups, to become the fastest growing in the nation. He has electrified audiences around the world with his wit, high-octane public speaking. His mission in life is to prove that every business can be phenomenally successful online, with the right tools and knowledge. Doyle has an MBA in Leadership and is the author of two books on digital leadership, brand strategy and online marketing.

He is a leading innovator in the online, e-commerce world. He has helped businesses grow and achieve their goals through harnessing their knowledge, expertise and entrepreneurial spirit. He has also presented and keynoted at numerous marketing and technology seminars in Canada, Australia and the United States.

Major work projects include e-commerce, web development, Search Engine Optimisation, Social Media Marketing, Social Media Training, Search Engine Marketing, and Online Advertising.

Currently, as a digital strategy and online marketing professional consultant, he is creating exciting and compelling digital-focused marketing strategies and implements them with quality, consistency and professionalism.

He teaches insights into digital marketing, including training in social media, as well as entrepreneurship and business planning. He writes for some blogs on business, strategy, online marketing, web business, digital media, social media, trends and subjects of interest to all entrepreneurs.

Education is the core of what he does, including teaching at the secondary level in Australia for Curtin University, as well as for several social groups in Canada, including a restitution program started by the University of Manitoba, and the John Howard Society.

Doyle was nominated for the Canadian Ernest C. Manning Innovation Award for software and operational systems that he managed and developed for his start-up businesses. He is the holder of two international patents for consumer products and online technology customization methods.

He was awarded his Masters of Business in 2002 for his Thesis on "Mass Customization in the Retail Consumer Environment", from Royal Roads University, in Victoria, Canada. This was the beginning of the entrepreneur adventure for Doyle, as it formed the basis of the subsequent business start-ups in the ensuing years.

One of the online businesses that he started and led, mytego.com, was named as "Profit Magazine's Hot 50 Fastest Growing Companies in Canada" in 2008, as well as the "Manitoba Business Magazine's #1 Fastest Growing Company" for the State, in 2009.

The digital framework that was developed for this book was also awarded the 2013 "Smart 100" Award for Innovation from Australian Anthill Magazine.

Doyle has always been actively involved in the business community, providing mentorship for new entrepreneurs for the Canadian Youth Business Foundation Program, Junior Achievement, as well as other collegiate entrepreneurship programs. He has also served on many Council and Entrepreneur Boards, as well as creating several distinctive Entrepreneur Business Networking organizations throughout Canada & Australia.

His online experience has been utilized in various global industries, including travel, fashion insurance, pharmaceuticals, banking, investment, hospitality, financial, events and learning domains.

Need additional details?

Feel free to send me an email: doyle@dept.digital

SPEAKING ENGAGEMENTS ON DIGITAL STRATEGY

Speaking Engagements On Digital Strategy, The art of disruption & Online Marketing

Doyle Buehler has electrified audiences around the world with his wit, wisdom and high-octane public speaking.

Doyle is at the intersection of digital innovation and entrepreneurship. He creates revolutionary frameworks that allow businesses to overcome the clutter and confusion and overwhelming information online. As he can clearly explain, businesses no longer need to worry about the intricacies of what to do online, because they have new, remarkable platforms that work for them, not against them. Through his presentations, workshops and speeches, he helps business leaders take back control of their businesses through his core digital strategies that create the breakthroughs that all businesses are looking to implement.

Doyle provides an enlightening, yet comprehensive framework of the specific details entrepreneurs and business leaders need to follow, implement and understand for the greatest level of business success online. Doyle helps every leader from those managing startups to those running the world's top firms navigate online marketing hype, distilling his methodology into a manner that is easy to understand so businesses can create new and revealing opportunities for businesses.

Want some new insights into digital marketing and online strategy for your audience? Please contact me via email doyle@dept.digital

Download my media kit here: www.dept.digital

#BREAKTHROUGH AUDIO BOOK VERSION

Get a free audiobook version of #Breakthrough to listen on the road, while you're traveling, just want to learn the quick and easy way, or in your most boring meetings.

Go to: Breakthrough.digital/audiobook

ACKNOWLEDGMENTS

Special Thanks To:

Andrew Griffiths, a wonderful mentor and best-selling author, who has guided my entire process. A true inspiration.

Daniel Priestly, Glen Carlson, and everyone at the Key Person of Influence Program who has helped me unleash and focus my entrepreneur strengths.

Andrew O'Connell, for his editorial support

Elly Sumich for her un-ending support, patience and understanding.

JOIN THE DIGITAL LEADERSHIP CHALLENGE

Start building out your #Breakthrough plan step by step, and be guided along the way. The #Breakthrough challenge helps you create the proper digital workflows that work best for your business.

www.breakthrough.digital/challenge

DID YOU ENJOY THE BOOK?

I really hope you've enjoyed the book, and that it was helpful and useful to you, in at least one small (or big!) way. I have a favour to ask you. Would you consider giving it a rating and review on Amazon, please? My goal is for this book to help as many businesses as possible, and to help them move beyond mediocrity. One way to help establish the book's status is getting some "Love" on Amazon, as to what is good about it.

So if you could be so awesome, head on over to Amazon, and leave a review for all to enjoy your kind words.

Just search by the title of the book.

Thanking you in advance,

Doyle Buehler

INDEX

READY TO #BREAKTHROUGH ONLINE WITH YOUR BUSINESS?

Many businesses and entrepreneurs have lost the real focus on what is really important about their business online. They're uncertain on how to create influence and how to deliver their unique brand value.

Do you know what to do "next", online, to propel your business forward? How do you create influence online? How can you get a thriving audience base, and more leads and sales from your online efforts?

It's not just about your website, nor "traffic"; it's not about your "followers", either. And no, it's not about being on Facebook and running some ads. This book is the next step in a digital transformation of your business, to deliver your remarkable brand value to your audience.

This is what I will show you, to help you reach your #Breakthrough Online for your business:

- How to create a compelling digital strategy that will answer the fundamental question of 'why', and how you will actually deliver your remarkable value online.

- What is really important about online marketing specifically for your business, and how to properly leverage it for your unique audience.

- How to build a reliable, strong, stable and superior platform for your own digital ecosystem, by utilizing a simple process and methodology.

- Define how to move your business from a simple transactional foundation to a transformational value offering that builds your digital authority.

Breakthrough.Digital

CPSIA information can be obtained
at www.ICGtesting.com
Printed in the USA
BVHW081616181218
535836BV00003B/261/P